# UNTIL
# MORNING
# COMES

A WORD OF HOPE AND PEACE
THROUGH THE NIGHT

# UNTIL MORNING COMES

Malcolm W. Coby, Ph.D.

TATE PUBLISHING & *Enterprises*

Published by Tate Publishing & Enterprises, LLC
127 E. Trade Center Terrace | Mustang, Oklahoma 73064 USA
1.888.361.9473 | www.tatepublishing.com

Tate Publishing is committed to excellence in the publishing industry. The company reflects the philosophy established by the founders, based on Psalm 68:11,
*"The Lord gave the word and great was the company of those who published it."*

Book design copyright © 2009 by Tate Publishing, LLC. All rights reserved.
*Cover design by Tyler Evans*
*Interior design by Lindsay B. Behrens*

Published in the United States of America

ISBN: 978-1-61566-411-5
1. Religion / Christian Life / Personal Growth
2. Religion / Christian Life / Death, Grief, Bereavement
09.11.19

# DEDICATION

God has released two wonderful vessels of honor into my life to whom this book is dedicated. Seldom is one blessed twice in life with such jewels. I dedicate this work to the memory of my high school sweetheart and loving wife for the first thirty-six years of my life, the late Annie Coby, who walked with me through valleys and inspired me to conquer mountains. I dedicate this work to my wonderful gift from God, Reva Coby, my precious wife for the rest of the journey, who brings an incredible strength through times of tears and laughter, and whom God has used to usher in the joy of morning to the rest of my life. I am certainly a grateful and blessed man. I also dedicate this work to my children: Lisa, Malcolm Jr., and Maria, whom I pray will be healed and blessed by the ministry of this publication.

# ACKNOWLEDGMENTS

I am grateful for the gift of the Holy Spirit, for it was through his inspiration and guidance that this publication was developed. I am also indebted to the following individuals who assisted in proofreading and offering constructive criticism for this work to develop properly: My wife, Reva Coby; David Chandler; Sarafia Fleming; Mary Surratt; and Angela Lewis. Appreciation is also extended to an admired colleague and friend, Bishop Jerry W. Macklin, for his invaluable advice and mentoring over the years.

# TABLE OF CONTENTS

# FOREWORD

So often, in this hurried world in which we live, we hear young people assailing the goal of destination, the importance of being there. However, as we grow in years and maturity we realize that it is not just *being there* that matters, but more often, it is the journey that matters even more. It is *getting there* that provides the joy and yes, even the pain that defines the business of living. However, *joy* cannot be fully appreciated without experiencing *pain*. How we embrace pain, loss, and disappointments impacts and directs the journey ahead. In this work, *Until Morning Comes,* Dr. Malcolm Coby comes to walk with us in our life's journey as he gives us insight into his own personal journey, having trod the valley of loss, encountering its inevitable pain, and through the wisdom of Scripture, discovered the profound, deep joy that follows.

A famous Chinese writer tells us there are two classes of authors: One will accumulate data, sort that data, and draw conclusions. The other kind, when faced with the same data, incorporates it into his or her life, and later is compelled to write by the urgency of that vital experience. In *Until Morning Comes*, Dr. Malcolm Coby has been compelled to write this wonderful work.

I have had the blessed privilege of counting Dr. Malcolm Coby as a dear friend and colleague for more than thirty years. Like so many others, I have shared a great appreciation for his keen intellect and academic acumen as he has given himself to the pursuit of excellence in all that he does. While his colleagues and I have come to expect his contributions to be beneficial in the areas of organization and administration, we are most blessed in this new book by the costly fruit of this writer's pains, struggles, and joys.

With biblical insight and wisdom, Dr. Coby leads us ever so gently into the presence of our eternal Creator, whose love and comforting Spirit sooths our broken hearts, places our fears at peace, and helps us to see the rays of tomorrow's sun shining through the pain of our today. Yes, *Until Morning Comes* makes the journey more bearable.

Bishop J. W. Macklin

# INTRODUCTION

Life consists of events that could be categorized as either gains or losses. We gain life at the time of conception. At birth, we lose the safety of our mother's womb and enter the world with a cry for continued protection. As life goes on, the losses seem to outnumber the gains. We experience the loss of friends and acquaintances with whom we grew up, never to see again. We lose the innocence of childhood to the turmoil of adolescence. We lose the naiveté of immaturity to the realities of adult life. We lose parents and other loved ones through expected and unexpected death. We experience the loss of jobs and health. We lose relationships through divorce, abuse, or abandonment. All of this comes with the undeniable lesson that life is only temporary. The sagacious preacher declared, "To everything there is a season and a time to every purpose under the sun," (Ecclesiastes 3:1, KJV).

You are always in season as long as you live. You may not like the climate that accompanies winter, but thank God seasons do pass, and spring is soon to follow. You have but one lifetime to fulfill your purpose assigned by God. However, during your life you will experience all of the above-mentioned losses but must continue to fulfill your purpose on this earth. When tragedies of any nature occur, we often receive the well-intentioned advice that "things will get better in the morning." In the meantime, you still have the pain and grief associated with the loss. The key question is, "What will you do until morning comes?" That is what this book is about.

This book may be used as a resource for funeral sermons. More importantly, as was the case for this author, it may be used by anyone who has experienced a loss in his or her life. It is designed to bring consolation to the hearer or the reader based on the Word of God. You will discover that joy does not come just because it is morning. Joy ushers in the morning. This writer's prayer is that as you read you will be blessed until (your) morning comes.

Bishop Malcolm W. Coby, B.S., M.ED., Ph.D.

# UNDERSTANDING
# THE NIGHT

In Psalm 30, David praises God for delivering him and encourages others to praise him. He remembers his former security and his prayer when he was in trouble. This was a psalm and song sung with the voice to the tune of instruments at the dedication of the house of David. As he recalls his experiences of a dysfunctional family; the wrath of Saul; and the solace of his friend, Jonathan, he pens, "Weeping may endure for a night, but joy comes in the morning," (Psalm 30:5b, AMP).

Weeping is reserved for the night. Night is the hour of grief. It is a common experience. We have all experienced grief. We are familiar with the intensity of emotions associated with it. But do we all experience the same feelings each time we lose a loved one or get a divorce or lose a job or our health? Grief is generally defined as the cause of intense, deep, and profound sorrow, especially a specific event or situation. Most of the literature seems to point to the commonalities from the perspective of stages or phases of the night (grief). Perhaps the most well known of these might be from Elizabeth Kubler-Ross's book *On Death and Dying*[1]. In it, she identified five stages that dying patients experience when informed of their terminal prognosis.

The stages Kubler-Ross identified are: 1) denial (This isn't *happening* to me!); 2) anger (Why is this happening to *me?*); 3) bargaining (I promise I'll be a better person *if*... 4) depression (I don't *care* anymore); 5) acceptance (*I'm ready* for whatever comes). These phases, rather than stages, are evident in the behaviors of those who experience grieving situations also. The word *stages* suggests that one must move in a hierarchal fashion from one to the next. The truth is that one may go from bargaining to acceptance and back to anger and depression. There is no evidence of a predictable pattern that will fit all people. There is no script for the night. The only thing that is certain is that the night will come.

Dr. Roberta Temes, in her book *Living with an Empty Chair: A Guide Through Grief*[2], describes three particular types of behavior exhibited by those suffering from grief and loss.

1.  numbness (mechanical functioning and social insulation)

2. disorganization (intensely painful fe loss)

3. reorganization (reentry into a more "normal" social life)

This perspective has some salient features. One is the visibility of the phases in one's life. The road to healing begins with recognition of the nature of the pain. It allows some prescription for recovery by analyzing the type of nonproductivity involved in the first two and the hope evidenced by the last.

Grief, the night, is individualized and cannot be reduced to a simple list. It is as individual as the one who experiences it. There is no quick fix. It is complex in its resolution. There is no one prescription. The resolution of grief is not an event but a process. Just as we have different emotional reactions to anything that happens in our lives, so too will we experience grief and loss in different ways.

The important thing to remember is that there is a wide range of emotions that may be experienced. One must also understand that the feelings will occur. Keep them in perspective. Seek to understand why you feel a certain way. If there are any unresolved issues that cause particular emotional pain, forgive yourself and others and, if necessary, talk with someone about it.

## Joy Brings the Morning

There is no scheduled completion date to grieving. The Word of God only assures us that it only came for the night. No one can define the length of your night. Unresolved grief only lengthens the night. Work through your night as effectively as you can, using prayer, counseling, support groups, etc. The scripture says that joy comes in the morning. Morning represents a new day. How does it come? This writer submits to you that the morning is not automatic. It is not simply a matter of time. It is a matter of faith and work. Have faith in God and his Word. I submit to you that joy brings the morning. The prophet declared that the joy of the Lord is our strength. Joy is more than an emotion. It is a choice. The night can silence your joy if you let it. This book is an attempt to assist you in ushering in your morning. The Apostle Paul advised in Philippians 4:6–8:

> Do not fret or have any anxiety about anything, but in every circumstance and in everything, by prayer and petition (definite requests), with thanksgiving, continue to make your wants known to God. And God's peace [shall be yours, that tranquil state of a soul assured of its salvation through Christ, and so fearing nothing from God and being content with its earthly lot of whatever sort that is, that peace], which

transcends all understanding, shall garrison and mount guard over your hearts and minds in Christ Jesus. For the rest, brethren, whatever is true, whatever is worthy of reverence and is honorable and seemly, whatever is just, whatever is pure, whatever is lovely and lovable, whatever is kind and winsome and gracious, if there is any virtue and excellence, if there is anything worthy of praise, think on and weigh and take account of these things [fix your minds on them]. (AMP)

# A BETTER DAY

Scripture Text: Joel 2:28

Focus: Hope

The theme of disaster is found throughout the book of Joel—locusts, plagues, famine, raging fires, invading armies, etc. However, the promises of hope are interspersed with the pronouncements of coming judgment. The message of Joel is clear: if you think a plague of locusts is bad, wait until you see the final judgment of the Lord. But things are not always as bad as they seem. Every true child of God knows not to stop with the prediction of doomsday. God will also send a day of grace. That grace is sufficient for a better day.

Joel prophesied at a time of great devastation to the entire land of Judah. An enormous plague of locusts had covered the countryside and eliminated all of the vegetation. It destroyed the pastures of both the sheep and the cattle. It even stripped the bark off the fig trees. In just a few hours, what was once a beautiful and fruitful land had become a nightmare in front of their eyes. The plague recorded in this book was greater than anyone had ever seen. All the crops were lost, and the seed crops for the next planting season were also destroyed. A terrible famine had seized the entire land. In fact, it had killed both people and animals. There was a great need for hope in a hopeless time.

Sometimes you long for some relief, and none seems to come your way. Your search may seem in vain. There are projects and plans you set in motion that may not change soon enough to cultivate your faith. You gave your life to Christ, and there is still no answer from the Lord. However, the Lord has a promise in his Word that cannot be denied. "Many are the afflictions of the righteous: but the Lord delivereth him out of them all," (Psalm 34:19, KJV). God will do just what he says. He is God and cannot lie.

The reality of life is that it is filled with days. He told us in the language of the wise preacher, "In all thy ways acknowledge him, and he shall direct thy paths." In the original language, the word *ways* meant all of your recurring moments of time. That is exactly what a day is all about. So life is filled with days. Some days seem good, and some days seem bad. A day is a measurable span of time. It means more than a twenty-four-hour period. It is a period of existence. A good day could be considered a day of strength. It is a day of victory and triumph. It is a day of deliverance. It is a day of receiving mercy from God.

Then there are bad days. A bad day is especially bad when God is not in your life. It is a time of sorrow. Sorrow is born out of regret. We have regrets when we realize that there are those things we should have done when we had the opportunity. When that opportunity is missed or ignored, we enter into a day of judgment. If we get stuck in the judgment mode, we will miss the redemption of God. Has God given you directions you did not follow? Has he called you, and you did not come? Has he tried to turn you around, and you would not turn? It is not the wrath of God that is summoning you to him. It is his loving-kindness that is drawing you near to him. Believe it or not, God wants you to have a better day.

When is that day coming? The day of darkness will pass. The locusts will die or fly away. The torrid sun will set in the west. The persistent rain will stop. It may seem like you have been abandoned. Your better day will not be announced. Yes, weeping may endure for the night, but joy is coming in the morning. The morning will not be announced by the crowing of the rooster or the sounding of the alarm clock. It comes when you reach that point of decision that God and you are in charge of your destiny. What we have to do is turn our troubles and cares over to the Lord. In fact, he told us to cast them on him simply because he cares for us. If you are in sin and in the judgment of God, he is the only one who can cancel that kind of day.

A better day is more than just another good day when most things go well rather than sour. It is that day when you know that you know without really knowing that everything will be all right. A better day has been promised to each of us.

Joel looked down through time and heard the promises of Jesus, who said, "I will pray the Father to send you another Comforter. He saw and heard the Lord saying to us today. And it shall come to pass afterward, that I will pour out my spirit upon all flesh; and your sons and your daughters shall prophesy, your old men shall dream dreams, your young men shall see visions: And also upon the servants and upon the handmaids in those days will I pour out my spirit" (Joel 2:28–29, KJV).

God said he would pour out his Spirit. This signifies the great abundance of God. He is El Shaddai (more than enough). He is not pouring out all of his Spirit except for what you and I need to have. God sent enough rain to restore the parched land and fill up the dried streams. Some people come to God for a little touch. You need to know that what is coming out of God for you is a "pour out." He also said that if you believe in him as the Scriptures have said, out of your belly (inward parts) shall flow rivers of living waters. You do not have to wait for the pour out of God; you are in it right now. When your faith and the will of God meet, there will be an outpour.

God is no respecter of persons. Your sorrow does not have to be greater than anyone else for God to pour out on you. He said he would pour out on all flesh; that is, every class of people. An individual that misses the outpour will not miss it because of nationality or race or color but because he or she has not surrendered that life to Jesus Christ. Surrender and walk in the light, as he is in the light. In times of trouble, loss, and turmoil, allow him to lead you beside still waters. That is where he wants to restore your soul (mind, will, and emotions). He wants your mind to be the mind of Christ. He wants you to surrender your will to his will. He also wants your emotions to be at peace.

When God blesses you with a better day, it reaches beyond you. He is blessing the nation that comes from you. He is setting up your children and children's children to be the ones who will rise up and bless the name of the Lord. A prophet is one who speaks forth what God is saying. God needs somebody who is willing to share the good news with a dying world. The harvest is ready, but the laborers are few. Can God trust you as a laborer?

For those in their golden years, God is not through with you yet. You are not too old to have a better day. Job's testimony was that for all the days of his appointed time, he would wait until his change came (a better day) (Job 14:14). Also, you cannot be too young for God to use you. The youth of our nation are an endangered species. God will use you if you will stop trying to fit in with everyone else's plans but his. Until morning comes, stop trying to impress people who simply do not care or will not remember your name at the ten-year class reunion.

Finally, there are those whom society seems to shun. Joel included even the lowest strata of society: the slaves. God said he would also pour out his Spirit on them. Nowhere in the Old Testament is there even one instance of a slave functioning as a prophet. God uses ordinary people to do his will. He used the lunch of a little boy to feed thousands of men, women, and children. However, the first requirement was for the lad to give up his lunch.

I am sure he promised his mother that he would not waste the food but never thought that a grown man, especially a teacher, would ask him for it. What would he tell his mother when he returned home? But consider the believability of the story he did tell her when he and his friends brought home twelve baskets of bread and fish!

If you want a better day, you will have to get ready to give up something. Jesus summoned, "Come unto me, all ye that labour and are heavy laden, and I will give you rest. Take my yoke upon you, and learn of me; for I am meek and lowly in heart: and ye shall find rest unto your souls," (Matthew 11:29–29, KJV). In order to take his yoke, you have to give up what yours. What do you have that is keeping you from having a better day? Perhaps it is anger, bitterness, past sins, or failures. Perhaps it is time to release them into the hands of Jesus. He wants you to have rest from struggling with a situation that is completely out of your control. Let it go and rest.

Yes, there is rest for the people of God, but it is not just when you get to heaven. The Scriptures tell us to labor to enter into that rest. That rest is the place or condition of complete satisfaction with the will of God. You must trust him whether you understand his will or not. Someone said in a song, "Take your burdens to the Lord and leave them there. If you trust and never doubt, He will surely bring you out. Take your burdens to the Lord and leave them there."

The thief (Satan) wants to steal, kill, and destroy. He wants to steal the only thing that nobody can give or sell to you: time. He wants to kill your influence by keeping you under the cloud of gloom, and he wants to destroy your place in eternity. Jesus came that you may have life and that you may have it more abundantly. Enjoy your life today, and have a better day tomorrow.

# BEARING THE
# UNBEARABLE

Scripture Text: 1 Corinthians 10:13 and John 15:1–8

Focus: Strength and Resilience

No one knows the need for strength like a mother in labor. What seems to be unbearable turns to be sheer joy. Those who give up in life because of situations that seem unbearable need to gain strength from the Lord.

Who can you think of that has a job that is greater than any president, smarter than any teacher, wiser than any judge, more important than any physician, prettier than any queen, yet stronger than any athlete? Mothers are like that and more. They are people of special strength, passion, and sense of duty. Without mothers, there would be no next generation.

God illustrated the importance of mothers when he prepared for his Son, Jesus, to be born. He prepared a young virgin named Mary and highly favored her role. The greatest woman of all time was also the most humble of women. The first mother, Eve, was the vehicle for the manner of childbirth, pain, and agony. However, Mary brought a special blessing one night to a dying world in a humble stable in Bethlehem. "Away in a manger no crib for a bed, the little Lord Jesus lay down his sweet head." And caressing the King of kings was his mother, Mary.

How could she bear not being in a private room at the local obstetrics hospital? Where were the lace curtains and matching carpet? Besides all of that, there were no attendants, orderlies, nurses, or physicians—not even a midwife. But she had made a commitment to God and sent a message back to heaven by the same angel: "and Mary said, 'Behold the handmaid of the Lord; be it unto me according to thy word.'"

God chose a mother to do what no one on earth could do. Besides bearing the Son of God, she bore the burden of being misunderstood. Don't forget that God had said something special about her. She was highly favored among women. God had picked her out for a task that he would not entrust to anyone else. What a compliment that was to her! When God picks you out for a task, rest assured you are suited for the task, whether you know it or not. He will make a way for you to bear what you think is too heavy for you.

Remember his Word: "No temptation [trouble] has seized you except what is common to man. And God is faithful; he will not let you be tempted beyond what you can bear. But when you are tempted, he will also provide a way out so that you can stand up under it" (1Corinthians 10:13, NIV). In other words, if you have it, you can handle it. God said that! (Note: I want to substitute the word *trouble* for *temptation*. Trouble is the catalyst that leads to the temptation to not trust God.)

When faced with life's difficulties, you have to stop allowing the enemy of God to dictate what you can and cannot handle. Paul describes the challenge as a temptation. Another word for it is *trouble*. Although they are not synonymous, they both attempt to serve the same purpose. That purpose is to distract you from the will of God and deny you the victory you deserve. The bottom line is that God has already said that you can bear it. So what makes it so unbearable?

The enemy of God would have you avoid as much trouble as possible. He would deceive you into thinking that you are doing all right because you have shunned the challenges in your life. It is like defining success as the lack of failure. The lack of failure exists because of the lack of attempting the challenge.

Jesus said, "These things I have spoken unto you, that in me ye might have peace. In the world ye shall have tribulation: but be of good cheer; I have overcome the world," (John 16:33, KJV). Unbearable situations are often found in the fundamental elements of life. It may include poverty, sickness, financial difficulties, and other normal pressures of life. That is the bad news. The good news is that we do not have to worry about the bad news, because through Jesus we are more than conquerors.

Yes, as in the case of Job, God allows some trouble, but God never sends us trouble. "Let no man say when he is tempted, I am tempted of God: for God cannot be tempted with evil, neither tempteth he any man: But every man is tempted, when he is drawn away of his own lust, and enticed," (James 1:13–14, KJV). Isn't it interesting that some people are drawn to trouble rather than away from it? Perhaps it is due to guilt or a sense of unworthiness, but it is totally unnecessary.

Sometimes, any kind of trouble seems unbearable. This is especially true when it comes to us again and again. We begin to describe such situations as inevitable occurrences. What seems unbearable is insufferable. Suffering is lonely. When you suffer, you do so all by yourself. No one can help you with it, and that seems unbearable.

The unbearable is that which has become excruciatingly painful with no relief in sight. It is agonizing and seems to engulf your entire being. If you are not careful, it will begin to create hatred and bitterness in your spirit. Normal situations to others can become emotionally intolerable.

The unbearable does not become unbearable by choice. It becomes unbearable after you have done all you can to bear it, or at least you think you have done all you can. The truth is you have not begun to draw from the power that is within you. Remember, you are more than a conqueror through he who loved you (Romans 8:37). Christ has conquered the enemy already.

The real decision is to bear or not to bear. Why bear a burden or trouble? Is it worth it? Why have all of that on your shoulders? Why even try to hold up under the pressure? Why continue to carry on as if everything is all right? The Word of God always has the appropriate answer. "Be not afraid nor dismayed by reason of this great multitude; for the battle is not yours, but God's" (2 Chronicles 20:15b, KJV). God cannot lie. Depend on what he has already said.

Until morning comes, we must realize that there are some things that God will not do. First, he will not make the devil leave you alone. You still have to resist him. Before Satan will flee from you, you must submit yourself to God. You must surrender your faith in God and keep it focused on God and not your situation. Deliverance is often a process instead of an event.

Secondly, God will not make you know the Bible. You still have to read it and study it for yourself. If you want freedom from sorrow, you must first know what the truth is from the Word of God. John said in chapter 8 verse 32, "And ye shall know the truth, and the truth shall make you free" (KJV). Only the truth that you know (understand) will make you free. Anyone can be set free and still not be completely free. He or she cannot maintain that freedom. Complete freedom comes when you accept and understand the truth. Complete freedom does not mean that the reality of the sorrow or situation has somehow disappeared. However, it results in God lifting you above the impact of the situation. You will still see what you see, know what you know, and remember what you remember. Faith in God is what lifts you above the situation.

Finally, God will not send somebody else to remove afflictions. James wrote, "Is any among you afflicted? Let him pray. Is any merry? Let him sing psalms," (James 5:13, KJV). The point is that the first step of the journey to strength is that you take the responsibility to move in that direction. Afflictions are not the same as illnesses. James said if you are sick, call for the elders of the church for prayer and anointing with oil. An affliction is a spiritual attack. The word is pictured in the New Testament as a beast of burden being crushed beneath a load that is just too heavy. It is also the picture of a person having a heavy weight placed on his chest and being pressed and crushed to the point that he feels he is going to die.

When you are attacked, the Word directs us to pray (James 5:13)! Pray for the strength of God to be activated. Pray for strength to bear what seems unbearable. In fact, the Word of God has already declared that you are able to bear it. Listen to what God says in two versions:

> There hath no temptation taken you but such as is common to man: but God is faithful, who will not suffer you to be tempted above that ye are able; but will with the temptation also make a way to escape, that ye may be able to bear it.
>
> 1 Corinthians 10:13 (KJV)

> No temptation has seized you except what is common to man. And God is faithful; he will not let you be tempted beyond what you can bear. But when you are tempted, he will also provide a way out so that you can stand up under it.
>
> 1 Corinthians 10:13 (NIV)

You must know that you are able to bear any testing that God permits and any affliction that comes from the enemy of God. God will provide a means of escape from any trouble or affliction that Satan puts in your way. God will provide an escape route in the midst of the trouble. You may not see the way out immediately, but if you will trust in God, pray, and seek the wisdom of God, freedom is guaranteed.

You cannot have strength to overcome anything if you are not connected to a source of strength. Be certain that you are connected to the only source that can provide what you need: Jesus. He is El Shaddai. He is more than enough. He is the all-sufficient one.

Jesus described his sufficiency in terms that fruit growers could understand. He said that he is the True Source (True Vine) and his Father is the Farmer. If we are grafted into the vine, we will begin to bring forth the kind of fruit that will give life. The truth is that a branch that is not attached to the True Vine will not be able to bring forth any fruit or signs of life on its own. He then made it clearer when he said that God is glorified when we abide in him and his words abide in us. Then we have the privilege and strength to bear the unbearable. "If ye abide in me, and my words abide in you, ye shall ask what ye will, and it shall be done unto you," (John 15:7, KJV).

Regardless of the type of loss or devastation, God has spoken. Paul understood it when he said in Philippians 5:13, "I can do all things through Christ which strengtheneth me." All things include the unbearable. Whatever is unbearable for those who do not know Christ is bearable for those of us who know him. We know that we do not bear these burdens alone. Jesus will help us, and Jesus alone.

Let us conclude with the words of consolation and direction from one who experienced many of life's unbearable situations. Many of these came from within his own family. David wrote:

The Lord is my light and my salvation; whom shall I fear? The Lord is the strength of my life; of whom shall I be afraid? When the wicked, even mine enemies and my foes, came upon me to eat up my flesh, they stumbled and fell. Though a host should encamp against me, my heart shall not fear: though war should rise against me, in this will I be confident. One thing have I desired of the Lord, that will I seek after; that I may dwell in the house of the Lord all the days of my life, to behold the beauty of the Lord, and to inquire in his temple. For in the time of trouble he shall hide me in his pavilion: in the secret of his tabernacle shall he hide me; he shall set me up upon a rock. And now shall mine head be lifted up above mine enemies round about me: therefore will I offer in his tabernacle sacrifices of joy; I will sing, yea, I will sing praises unto the Lord.

Psalm 27:1–6 (KJV)

When faced with unbearable situations, sacrifice the very thing that, at that time, you have in short supply: praise. If you will sacrifice the little praise you have left, more praises will come to you. Notice that the psalmist did not say he felt like praising but made it his choice. He said, "I will sing praises." Praise in times of unbearable situations is not based on whether it is appropriate or not. It is a matter of your will. Will you sing? Will you praise God? The choice is yours. You will find that praise begets praise. The more you praise him, the more you will want to praise him.

Remember this:

If God brings you to it,

He will bring you through it.

Happy moments, praise God.

Difficult moments, seek God.

Quiet moments, worship God.

Painful moments, trust God.

Every moment, thank God.

# DISCOVER PEACE

Scripture Text: Luke 19:41–42

Focus: Peace

This is more than a word about peace. It is a treatment of the issue of breakthrough to discovery. Discovery is not the same as creation. Creation is the making of something that did not exist before. Discovery is finding what is already there. No one created gold; they just discovered gold. No one created oil; they just discovered where the oil was located. God created everything on the earth. Humans just discovered it.

Peace. Discover peace! It is the discovery of the right kind peace that makes it effective and valuable. There were those in the days of the gold rush in the 1840s that discovered gold only to find out it was fool's gold. It was gold that was not as valuable as they initially thought. Somebody may think he or she is living under the banner of peace and that everything is satisfactory. I invite you to join this expedition to the land of peace. See if you can discover the kind of peace that only knowing Christ can bring to you and to me.

The sad commentary on this is that this peace is available every day to everyone. It is available in every situation; even when it seems like there is war, that peace is present. There have been times in the heat of the battle that soldiers have faced one another all alone, knowing that the orders were that when they find the enemy, kill him. Somehow they made an inaudible decision that today they were going to be at peace.

Every time the enemy fires a weapon, there is an opportunity to be at peace, but when that weapon is out of ammunition, the decision has to be made whether to reload or not. Unfortunately, there have been too many people reloading in the home. They have reloaded to attack with one more unnecessary word when silence would have ended the war. Instead of saying, "I'm sorry. Forgive me," they reloaded and missed the opportunity that was present for peace.

This fruit of the Spirit called peace is a rather unusual commodity in the life of the child of God because it is fruit that continues to grow. It is an inexhaustible aspect of the power of God, allocated only to those who know how to wisely use it. You will discover in this passage of Scripture that peace was available, but they refused to use it, refused to own it, refused to claim it, and even refused to recognize it.

Consequently, that which is not claimed stops growing. There are times when you must make peace. The Bible says, "Blessed are the peacemakers for they shall be called the children of God," (Matthew 5:9, KJV). Every time you make peace, there is an opportunity to grow more peace out of your spirit. You become more tolerant of situations that you could not tolerate before. But if you refuse to let the peace develop within you, it's like a beautiful tree I had when we lived on 42nd street in Oklahoma City. I had a beautiful plum tree in the backyard. Plums grew there so bountifully you could just smell them when you opened the door. We said, "Well, tomorrow we will get the plums." When tomorrow came, the birds got to them first, and what the birds didn't get, the worms ruined, and there were no more plums. And so it is with the peace that God says grows from my Spirit. Like the plums, that which is neglected is often exposed to destruction. The enemy of God will attack that which has great value. Peace is not only produced through you but has to be harvested and used to the glory of God.

The Spirit of God brings to us the legacy that Jesus left for us, according to St. John 14:27: "Peace I give unto you, I leave with you this peace. Not as the world giveth, give I unto you." It is the legacy of Christ. He said, "I'm giving you such an unusual fruit, that every time that you use it, it will grow again. And it will grow more abundantly. It will grow in a stronger fashion, and a more lasting manner." Additionally, every time you release peace, it develops an inner strength. Every time you release peace when you could have released war, and even rightfully so in some cases, you develop the fruit of the Spirit within you that makes you a stronger individual. It is a fruit that must grow in life. God wants you to live a peaceful life in a world full of chaos and trouble. Paul warned Timothy that these perilous times would come.

Unfortunately, even children of God view peace in such a shallow fashion that we often miss it. Peace is not just the absence of trouble. The fact that there is no trouble is not synonymous with peace. It may mean a break or it may mean a rest, but that does not mean there is peace. Peace in the Old Testament came from the word *Shalom,* which meant freedom from trouble. There is a powerful difference between absence of trouble and freedom from trouble. You can have trouble absent and not be free from it because you are still bothered about a situation. But when you are free of trouble even in the midst of trouble, you're not impaired by that trouble. Even in the midst of the trouble, in the midst of the attack, in the midst of the violence, and in the midst of the evil, you are free from its effects on you.

Therefore, freedom, *Shalom,* is freedom from trouble. Interestingly enough, it was used as a greeting as well as for departure, declaring that I wish you freedom; I pray for you to enjoy the highest good in life, the very best, possess all of the inner good that is possible. It was saying, "As I greet you, I wish you peace, and I also leave with a wish of peace. May you be free from the effects of trouble." However, you must know that trouble visits all of our houses sooner or later. In one form or another, it is coming. Jesus said, "In this life you will have trouble." He called it tribulation, which is recurrent trouble. You will have trouble. It not only visits occasionally but quite often. But thank God for he who said, "Be of good cheer, I have overcome the world."

There are two kinds of peace mentioned in Scripture. First, there is a peace that Jesus mentioned. He said the world gives a certain kind of temporary peace through the behavior of escapism. If I could just get away from you, we are at peace. We do not apologize. We have not straightened it out. Just get out of my way, and we will be at peace. But sooner or later we have to cross paths. If it is no more than in the line at convenience store, we may cross paths at some time or another.

The world says peace is to avoid trouble. How many times have families played the "Everything Is All Right" game? In David Field's book, *Family Personalities*[3].

he describes the kind of family that tends to be ideal. Everything seems okay on the surface. They come to church. They smile. They greet people. But all the way home, you see them all staring straight ahead. They don't talk to one another unless they are trying to say something good. They say good things to one another because they know that is what they want to hear, but the things that they don't say make them not a family. The things that they hold within are destroying the peace they think they have. Their definition of peace is to ignore the real issue. They hide their real feelings to avoid further trouble.

You can stir up trouble without ever saying a word. Avoiding trouble does not mean there is peace. And there are too many people in an estranged relationship assuming or pretending that they are at peace when they are just really putting up with each other. Subsequently, in that kind of family, children usually leave early and seldom come back. They never really learned to be at peace with each other. They never really put their arms around each other and said, "I love you" or "I care about you." They never discovered peace in the walls of their own home, so the world has a peace that is steeped in denial.

The Scriptures tell us about the peace that only the Lord can bring. One writer refers to it as bosom peace. It is not superficial. It's in my bosom. It's on the inside. It's peace that's within me; it's peace that is deep within that brings peace to my mind. It brings about certain composure. It is not just an attitude but also a composure. It represents a mindset that no matter how strong the winds are blowing, I am at peace. It does not matter how much trouble is in my heart or in my life, in my body, or in my situation—I am at peace. It is not the peace of denial because it realizes the storm is not over. While the storm is raging, I've declared peace. It is easy to declare peace to be still. I believe when Jesus said that, he was not only talking to the wind, he was talking to the disciples. He was saying, "You need to be still. You need to be at peace. You need to discover the stillness that peace brings." Bosom peace is a peace that settles and strengthens. Even in the most terrible situations and circumstances, it is more than just feelings and more than just attitude. It is a state of being. To be at peace is to have "bosom peace."

Thirdly, the peace of God is a peace of conquest. It is the peace of having conquered. It is the peace of the victor. Before the fight has started, there is a peace that represents contentment. There is a peace that neither sorrow nor danger nor suffering can take away, because regardless of what the score is, I win. Regardless of how soundly I seem to be defeated, I have the peace of conquest because I am more than a conqueror.

This is the peace of a victorious life. Again, Jesus said, "I'm leaving this with you. I'm going away but I'm going to leave you this legacy." You are going to be known by your love. You are going to be known by your composure. In the face of danger, in the face of lack, in the face of want, in the face of trouble, you are going to have the peace of conquest that I am giving to you, not as the world gives. Therefore, let not your hearts be troubled; neither let them be afraid. You can't really serve God in fear. You really can't pray well in fear. Some people come to the prayer meeting in a time of desperation, but sometimes that is the worst time to come. You ought to come long before then because you can develop peace. Often people will seek prayer and are desperately praying because the burden is so heavy. That it is not a prayer of faith but a prayer of fear.

In the book of Hebrews, chapter 4, verse 14, God says to come boldly to the throne of grace. Come with confidence. Don't come with fear. Come with confidence so you can find rest for your soul. Don't let your heart be troubled. Bosom peace is a peace of perfect assurance. It reproduces a peace of unquestionable confidence. There is a relationship that you can develop with God that your confidence in him is without question. You can say to yourself, *God I don't understand this, but I am at peace. In fact, I am not actually trying to understand this.*

The peace of assurance is a peace of a sure knowledge that my life or your life is in the hands of God. It is the peace of Romans 8:28, which says, "And we know that all things work together for the good, for the benefit of those who love the Lord and are the called according to His purpose." There are some things that will never make sense in life. Some things you just need to stop trying to understand and just trust God.

September 11, 2002 will never make sense in human terms. Some agnostics and atheists and others try to confuse Christians and ask, "Why did God let that happen?" All we know is that all things work together. In the sovereignty and the wisdom of God, we have no idea what those victims might have faced five months from then or a year from then or any other time. God didn't do it in the first place; therefore, asking God a question of why is an act of futility. Some things you just have to leave in the hands of God. You may tell God you hurt because of that, or that his actions puzzle you, but you need to continue to trust him. Let me discover that peace of perfect assurance. Allow me to discover that peace of knowing without it making sense because I trust in God.

Finally, bosom peace, the peace that's within, is the peace of intimacy with God. The world cannot understand that. The devil can't figure out how you lasted this long. It is that intimacy that led Apostle Paul to inquire, "Who shall separate us from the love of God; who is it; who can identify it, or who is important enough; who is great enough; who is of such influence in my life that will tear me away from this love that is stronger than a brother's love?" Jesus said, "Greater love hath no man than this than he lay down his life for a friend." Paul said, "Who can separate me? Shall it be peril or nakedness or things present or things to come? If I'm hungry or naked, if I don't have what I need, lift me up, put me down, what is it? Who is it? I'm persuaded that in all these things. We're more than co-conquerors." Nothing shall be able to separate me. Intimacy with God is a peace of, "I am not going anywhere."

There is a peace about your relationship with God that settles your mind and strengthens your will because sometimes you have a mind but don't have the will. At other times, you have the will but don't have the mind. But God gives you the will and, to do his will, it is a peace that settles the heart. You must discover that peace. The tragedy of not making this discovery is that there are situations that will rob you of your peace and distract you from what you already have. The key is to get your eyes off of it because the situation is so terrible that you can't see peace. And it is unfortunate that many have missed it. Families have been destroyed, and lives have been taken away. Lives have been ruined because they did not see the presence of peace.

Peace is always born out of reconciliation. It is born out of the need to reconnect. If there is a need for peace, something has been disconnected. Our relationships between man and God, relationships between men and men, have been disconnected, and so peace implies reconciliation. Reconciliation implies that peace is broken and conflict exists. Peace always has to do with personal relationships. Even when countries reconcile and ask for peace, there are persons who have to go and negotiate that peace. Whether it is man's relationship to God or to one another, it has to do with the relationship. In order to discover this kind of peace, there are several things you and I must do. We must follow peace! From Hebrew 12:14: "Follow peace with all men, and holiness, without which no man shall see the Lord."

Following peace is not just hoping it happens. The term in this sense means to pursue it, to chase it down and grab it and make sure that it happens. You must pursue peace, because Jesus said, "Blessed are the peacemakers." In the midst of every conflict and in the midst of every trouble is the opportunity to make a discovery. That discovery is the most valuable commodity of peace. The only reason the relationship hurts is because you care. If you didn't care, you wouldn't care if he or she came home or not. If you didn't care, you wouldn't care if he or she brought a paycheck home or not. But you cared, so you cried, you wept, you agonized, and you stayed up late at night. In the midst of all of that trouble, there is enough love for peace to be discovered.

The devil wants to emphasize the pain and the wrong, cruelty, unfairness, and the injustice. In spite of it all, God says, "I want you to find peace!" If you are going to give God the glory with your life, you absolutely must discover peace. The real question is, "Are you willing to make that the discovery? How willing are you to dig into your spirit to be healed. How deep are you willing to dig into your spirit to find the peace the Jesus left you?" It is still there. You don't feel it, but it is still there. You don't even want to talk about it, but it is still there. It may have happened ten years or twenty years ago. It may have happened when you were six, but Jesus said, "I've given you a different lifestyle now. You have peace."

The word in the New Testament for peace means the peace that binds us together. It means to weave together. You cannot weave together being distant. When Jesus died men had access to weave a relationship with God. When weaving takes place, we have peace with God. Are you willing to bind together hearts that have been distant? Are you willing to be joined together with God and with others? Don't wait too long. The longer you delay being at peace with your neighbor, being at peace with your brother or your sister or your relative, the more difficult it is to hear from God.

## Pain Brings Strain in Relationships

The Bible tells us in Genesis 45 that there was a man named Joseph who had been mistreated by his brothers, who were jealous of him. All he talked about was his dream, and in his dream Joseph's older brothers were bowing down to him. This young man had been mistreated and falsely accused of attempted rape by his employers and cast into prison. Finally God brought him up to be governor over all the land of the supply house. One day, into his office came these young men whom he recognized, but they didn't recognize him.

The Bible then records that he wept, and an Egyptian saw him crying. His tears were because he missed the peace they had as brothers.

Now here is the discovery of peace from Genesis 45:4: "And Joseph said unto his brethren, 'Come near to me, come near to me, come on brothers, don't stay over there, come near to me. I have no weapons to harm you. Come near to me.'" But they distanced themselves because of what had happened. There is a situation you cannot go back and fix—that is, if you knew how to fix it. You can change it by faith, by calling those things that are not as though they were.

Regardless of the situation, the voice of restoration and peace says, "Come near to me." Joseph was saying, as we should say, "Come near, because I've got something to release to you. I've got to release love in spite of what you've done to me."

There is nothing that we cannot do when we get near each other. Apart, we are messed up, and the enemy comes between us. There are too many families so distant in the same house. Somebody has to be brave enough to say, "Come near to me." Because when we release love, we release compassion, peace, and forgiveness. Forgiveness will bless you as much as it will bless your enemies. The fact that it does will bless you more because you don't have to carry that burden around any longer. Perhaps you need to make a phone call tonight or this evening and say, "Come near to me! I know we have not talked in a long time, but come near to me. It's all right now." I don't want to know why. Quit asking why. Why just opens more doors. Leave why alone, and just call them near to your heart. And with a sincere heart, the same God that released you will release the other people. As you release them, God releases you the more. He said, "How could I forgive you your trespasses if you don't forgive each other their trespasses?"

A time will come when another storm comes in your life. Storms will come in your life that you cannot hush. You cannot silence them and will not know what to do. There will be winds that will blow water all in your little boat, and it seems like the boat of existence is going down for the last time, but God said that there is a peace that you will discover in the midst of your own trials. And like the disciples who were on the sea, Jesus just simply said, "Peace be still." Be still.

# GOD'S BUSINESS

Scripture Text: Romans 9:10–13

Focus: Destiny/Unanswered Questions

Why does one person survive a disaster and another does not? Why did you survive a devastating situation? Why? So many questions of life go unanswered.

God is sovereign. He answers to no one. He does not have to explain himself. He does not owe you or anyone an explanation of what he chooses to do or allows to happen. God has a plan for mankind. He carried it out through his only begotten Son, Jesus Christ. His plan includes the reconciling of man to God through faith in Jesus Christ and his shed blood. It applies to everyone and anyone who will believe in him.

This leads us to the somewhat rhetorical question of why. Why are you here? Why did God take some, and others were left out of the same tragedy? The truth is that some things that happen simply do not make sense. The Word of God reminds us that everything works together for our benefit whether we understand it or not. This is especially true if we love God and accept that he has called us to a purpose in life. The Word goes on to tell us that God knew us before we were born for the purpose of being conformed to the image of his Son (Romans 8:28–29).

What is the plan of God for your life? Regardless of what has already taken place, God's plan will be ful-filled. We often question some of the things that have happened in our lives. Some we have chosen not to remember. There are things that have happened that we do not understand. God did not order everything that happened, but he used it in his plan to bring us to our purpose.

In spite of our failures, successes, wasted time, or whatever, God sent his son to die for us while we were yet sinners. In spite of our history, former lifestyles, personality flaws, shyness, timidity, God picked you out and approved you for a purpose before you were born.

Many of the people in the Bible whom God used the most had some undesirable traits. Moses had a speech problem, but God told him to tell Pharaoh to "let my people go." Timothy was scared, but he endured hardness as a good soldier of Jesus Christ. Peter had a hot temper, but Jesus trusted him to feed his sheep.

None were the most likely to succeed nominees of their time. God chose them all.

As we travel this journey of life, we must know that God knows how to take care of his business. We have to learn to trust him all along the way. Regardless of how difficult the circumstances or how unusual the situation, we must trust in him. He knows just what to do. Too often, we try to put God on the clock and get upset when he does not do what we want at the time we want. But we always need to remember that God is always on time; he is never too early or too late.

The psalmist wrote, "God is our refuge and strength, a very present help in trouble. Therefore will not we fear, though the earth be removed, and though the mountains be carried into the midst of the sea" (Psalm 46:1–2 KJV). God is always present. He chooses to be present. If we do not recognize his presence, the fact remains that he is present. We become more than conquerors because the battle belongs to God and not us. Trust him. He knows how to take care of business. Therefore, we must trust him with our future as well as with our current situation.

# IN HIS HANDS

Scripture Text: Jeremiah 18:1–6

    Focus: Sovereignty of God

This is a reminder of the power, strength, and tenderness that accompanies putting your life in the hands of the Lord. Regardless of our opinions, all things still work together for the good in our lives. Whatever the situation, put all things in his hands.

The text is a lesson from the Lord. The prophet Jeremiah is sent to the potter's house. He knew where to find it. He was not sent to preach a sermon. He was sent to receive a sermon already prepared. His only instruction was to go to the potter's house and observe how he manages his work. It was there that the Lord told the preacher that he would cause him to hear his words. In the wisdom of the Almighty, he orchestrates situations that will cause us to hear. Ironically, what we hear is what the Lord has been trying to convey to us all along. The potter's house experience was an illustration of God causing us to see what we need to hear.

The prophet was never disobedient to the words of the Lord but went straight to the potter's house. Take a closer look at what is happening. Imagine that we are now standing at the door of the potter's workshop. It is his factory where the water pots and vases and cooking and eating vessels are manufactured. It is a busy place quietly situated by the pools of Siloam in the Hinnon Valley. There is also a section for storing the clay. There is a place for the kiln for heating and hardening the clay. See the dump out in the back of the shop? That is the place for discarded vessels. Watch him now as he turns a heavy stone disc. He makes it look easy, giving constant movement to a lighter stone on top for the shaping of the clay.

As we step a little closer, we see that the first design of the vessel turns out misshaped. It seems worthless, because by now it is too small to be made like the others he was making. Then, almost without missing a beat, he quietly begins making and molding another vessel. God has the authority as well as the ability to form and fashion the great and the small as he pleases. He knows how to find those who will serve his purpose. It is a very easy thing for God to do what he pleases.

The message is clear. The clay simply responded to the strong but tender hands of the potter. It was crushed temporarily but reformed because of the marring as well as the reshaping. All of this happened while it was in his hands. This is the ultimate demonstration of faith and trust in the Potter. Whatever we are and whatever we have will be made as it should be when we put it in his hands. If we resist, we will become hardened and set, but the same gentle hands that molded us will become the hands of either restoration or chastisement.

To be in the hands of God means total trust in him. It requires a yielded spirit and an obedient heart. It is a position of dependency. This is a position that is often uncomfortable. We have such a high premium on our independence that we risk the blessings that accompany dependence on God. In times of difficulty and crisis, the worst thing we can do is try to be grown and independent. Christ has encouraged us to cast our cares (worries, fears, and intimidations) on him, for he cares for us. No matter how good or how bad circumstances may be, we still need the Lord. We need him always, period.

In the church, we often use the threat or cliché that there are people we will put in the hands of God. Sometimes it is said with the hope that God will do something to them that we think they deserve. When you put that unsaved loved one or unthankful child in the hands of God, do not be surprised if they get blessed. Be assured of this one thing: That which is committed to the hands of God is in safekeeping. Trust him to bring you through anything you are facing. He is sovereign. He does not have to explain what he is doing or what shall be the outcome. Surrender yourself to the hand of God and watch him work things out for you.

The glaring question of the day is, can I really release this to God? You must first determine what it is that must be released. What is released must remain with God if we are to see any valuable results. The interesting factor of the release is the waiting period. Yes, quite often, what you turn over to God he works for your good. You may or may not be ready for the results immediately when you release it. Isaiah instructs us, "But they that wait upon the Lord shall renew their strength; they shall mount up with wings as eagles; they shall run, and not be weary; and they shall walk, and not faint," (Isaiah 40:31, KJV). Waiting on the Lord is not a test of endurance or determination. Waiting has a purpose. The purpose of waiting is development. Development is defined as an incident that causes a situation to change or progress. This suggests that the very thing you want God to handle is an opportunity for you to change or make progress. What God knows is that you will need strength to accomplish what you have put in his hands.

Placing the situation in his hands will give you a new perspective. It is the perspective of the eagle. An eagle spends most of his time high above his situation. The circumstances and situations on the ground do not aggravate him. But from the ground, he soars to the mountaintop. When he has to change locations, he catches the wind and uses it to observe his situation. God wants you to soar above your situation on the wings of faith.

# LOOKING TO JESUS

Scripture Text: Hebrews 12:1

Focus: Focused Living

Life has many distractions. Distractions can be detrimental to holding on to eternal life. Looking to Jesus is the mission of every child of God to avoid missing the blessings he has in store for your life.

Life is the greatest race that you and I will ever run. The race for heaven, eternal life, knowing God, and fellowship with God all require a certain amount of discipline. No matter how long or short the race, everyone must endure until the end. We must not quit. We must not be so distracted that we stray from the path. We must not quit. The good news is that there are plenty of examples in the Word of God of those who stayed in the race. They serve as our inspiration. Winning the race has several key points to remember.

First, we must prepare to run. Preparation begins with knowing what you need as well as what you are holding onto that you do not need. The writer of the book of Hebrews put it this way: "Lay aside every weight…" The Greek term for weight is *ogkon panta*. It means everything legitimate. It even deals with the seemingly innocent things that may weigh you down. We must be aware of anything that does not build us up or make us stronger. Of course, the Word extends the list to those sins that keep recurring. It includes any ungodly behavior, habits, or whatever may be or will interfere with our winning the race.

Additionally, it includes many of the negative emotions and related baggage that often lingers or shows up out of nowhere to bring our spirits down. To lay aside such weights is to find a different place for them. Place them at a lower level of importance. This means it is your choice as to what you do with those mindsets. The Bible offers more specific directions for handling negative thoughts through the following passages:

> Casting down imaginations, and every high thing that exalteth itself against the knowledge of God, and bringing into captivity every thought to the obedience of Christ
>
> 2 Corinthians 10:5 (KJV)

> [Inasmuch as we] refute arguments and theories and reasonings and every proud and lofty thing that sets itself up against the [true] knowledge

of God; and we lead every thought and purpose away captive into the obedience of Christ (the Messiah, the Anointed One).

2 Corinthians 10:5 (AMP)

Secondly, we must run with discipline. Run with patience. This means pace yourself so that you do not burn out. Often, when the race seems long and dreary, there is a tendency to put forth a burst of speed only to discover that you do not have the stamina to finish the race. There are some situations that you hope and pray will end quickly. They may not. But God will use your patience to develop a strength that you could not get in any other manner.

The word *patience* is not a passive word. It is indeed active. It is how you run. It does not include sitting back and waiting to see what life has to dish out. It involves facing the longevity of undesirable situations with the faith of a patient and disciplined runner. A disciplined runner is not impressed or intimidated by how many runners pass by during the race. His focus is on the finish line.

To win the race, one must know what to do about distractions. Distractions are Satan's means of distracting the believer from the blessings of God. They may be in the form of sickness, family problems, emotional stress, etc. Although no two situations are exactly the same, there are some biblical principles involved that we can follow.

## How to Run a Race

This is not about how to run just any race but the race that is set before you. The race is your call to strength and healing. There is a prize. It is the prize of the high calling. God is calling you above your pain and loss. He is calling you to higher ground. Where you are right now may be dangerous. The ground is not stable. To reach the victory (the finish line or at least one of them) will require focus on the end at the beginning. In other words, the distractions and pains may come and go, but you must focus in the beginning of your dilemma and what you want things to be like at the end. The mental picture of victory will be the vehicle that God will use to keep you on course. The Bible confirms that how a man thinks in his heart, so is he (Proverbs 23:7a). The race to victory is toward the prize. How do we get there?

The imagery the Bible uses suggests an athletic contest in a great amphitheater. The witnesses are the heroes of the past who have just been mentioned (chapter 11). They are not spectators but inspiring examples. The Greek word translated *witnesses* is the origin of the English word *martyr* and means "testifiers, witnesses." They bear testimony to the power of faith and to God's faithfulness. Run with perseverance. The Christian life is pictured as a long-distance race rather than a short sprint.

Just as a runner concentrates on the finish line, we should concentrate on Jesus, the goal and objective of our faith (Philippians 3:13–14). Our faith, which has its beginning in him, is also completed in him. He is both the start and the end of the race. He is also the supreme witness who has already run the race and overcome. Joy sits before him. He is accomplishing our eternal redemption and his glorification at the Father's "right hand." He endured the cross. See Philippians 2:5–8. As with Christ, the humiliation of our present suffering for the gospel's sake is far outweighed by the prospect of future glory.

The key is knowing where to focus. The advice is "looking unto Jesus…" The idea is to look away from where you are looking to focus on the Lord. You must look away from the distractions of life to find the strength and peace in the name of Jesus. The practical application is the process of focusing on the Word of God. The trials of life often obscure the realities of the power of the written Word of God.

# MISSION ACCOMPLISHED

Scripture Text: Joshua 1:6–9

Focus: Destiny/Purpose for Living

Each person has a mission to fulfill. God wants each mission to be successful. Unfortunately, the steps toward making the mission successful are not always provided. The Word of God is the exception. God wants you to be successful. He rewards success. The great reward of eternal life is to hear the Lord say, "Mission accomplished."

In the scripture text, Joshua had just succeeded Moses as leader of the nation of Israel. Moses had led the nation for forty years and had the advantage of the wisdom and culture of Egypt and the king's house.

On the other hand, Joshua was relatively untried. He was assuming an awesome responsibility in taking command of two and a half million people. Certainly he needed a formula for success for this mission. Perhaps there were well-meaning people with good advice and formulas for success. Joshua had one trustworthy source: God himself.

God always calls us to a specific responsibility. He does not turn us loose in the world to search for some cause to which we can devote ourselves. He assigns us definite missions. We tend to generalize, but God is always specific. Before God calls one to great responsibility, he begins by giving him a great vision. He reveals what may be achieved. He opens the eyes of his people to what they can accomplish.

In the text, he revealed to Joshua the divine plan he had for the nation. It was a vision of what Israel could accomplish with and through him. Quite often, people are nearsighted as it relates relationship to the things of God. All the time they are planning, God has a design and plan for life that is so much greater than we realize. A most provocative question is, what would we be able to accomplish spiritually or naturally if we knew we could not fail? God never walks out on his promises or lets us down. The reason for life's unfilled missions is found in the fact that we have not fulfilled the conditions. One basic condition is that we hear him. We must keep our spiritual ears and eyes open to the matchless wisdom of God.

Another guideline for accomplishing the things of God is that we must seek the strength of God. Listen to the words of Joshua:

Be strong and of a good courage: for unto this people shalt thou divide for an inheritance the land, which I swore unto their fathers to give them. Only be thou strong and very courageous, that thou mayest observe to do according to all the law, which Moses my servant commanded thee: turn not from it to the right hand or to the left, that thou mayest prosper whithersoever thou goest. This book of the law shall not depart out of thy mouth; but thou shalt meditate therein day and night, that thou mayest observe to do according to all that is written therein: for then thou shalt make thy way prosperous, and then thou shalt have good success. Have not I commanded thee? Be strong and of a good courage; be not afraid, neither be thou dismayed: for the Lord thy God is with thee whithersoever thou goest.

Joshua 1:6–9 (KJV)

Notice that three times the instructions included exhortations to be strong and courageous. In fact, in the ninth verse, he gives the direct command to be strong and of a good courage—not a nervous courage but good (beneficial) courage. If the enemy cannot run you away from the battle, he will settle for you not paying close attention to your attitude of courage. He will distract you from your mission. That is when the twin enemies of doubt and fear take over. Paul wrote to the church at Ephesus (Ephesians 5:15–16) and told them to see that they walk carefully and take advantage of every opportunity to fulfill their mission. He recognized that time and conditions are like evil forces against the fulfillment of the will of God.

There must be no hesitation on our part. We must be willing to give ourselves completely to the assignment of God. We have no right to ask where and when we are coming out of a difficult dilemma. The fundamental issue is that we are willing to give ourselves completely to it. We must dare to venture out even in the face of impossible opposition. We must act as if we have nothing to lose and live as though nothing can stop us.

Allow me to submit five specific rules for accomplishing your mission. First, put God first. Matthew recorded Jesus as teaching, "Seek ye first the kingdom of God and His righteousness; and all these things shall be added unto you" (Matthew 6:33). Seeking the kingdom of God is not seeking a seat in heaven but seeking the rulership of God. The kingdom of God is where God rules. Does he rule in your heart and mind? That must first be firmly established before pursuing any kind of mission.

Secondly, follow the book. The elderly saints used to admonish the young to "do the Book." Regardless of how much excitement you have to serve the Lord, if you are not working according to the written will of God, you are just wasting your time. Verse eight in the text records Joshua saying that, "the law shall not depart out of my mouth; but thou shall meditate on it day and night." The rationale for this commitment was that it will lead to observing to do according to all that is written in it. The end result will be that you will prosper and have good success.

The third guideline is to seek or pursue the goal. Paul said that he may not have understood all of the lessons of life, but there is one thing that he learned that will definitely lead to a successful mission. He learned how to stop rehearsing the mistakes of the past. He learned to keep reaching for the goal that is set ahead. He called it the high prize of the calling of God in Christ Jesus. For your mission to be accomplished, you must keep your eyes on the prize. What is the prize? The prize is from your Commander in Chief. It is he who said, "Since you have been faithful over a few things, and I will make you ruler over many."

The next step is to never give up. Sounds trite and unnecessary, but it is vital. In the region of land known as Galatia, Paul told them, "And let us not be weary in well doing: for in due season we shall reap, if we faint not," (Galatians 6:9). There is no reward for half-accomplished missions. Furthermore, what good would it do? Who will be helped? Weariness is a given in Christian service. There will be seasons of fatigue and utter exhaustion. The motivation comes from two sources. One is the fact that reaping time follows service. The Lord said whatever is right will be paid. The second motivating factor is the love the servant has for his master. Jesus said, if you love me, you will keep my commandments. The commandments are not burdensome because of the love we have for the Lord.

The final component of success is the mindset that we accomplish our mission because we know we must do it all for the sake of Christ. Paul said that whatever happens he is doing it all for Christ. He said, "If I live, I have Christ, and if I die, I gain the presence of Christ." There is a certain amount of commendation that will come from others while you give the best of your service, but there is nothing close to the reward of hearing the Lord say, "Well done, thy good and faithful servant." Hear him say, "Mission accomplished."

# ONE OF A KIND

Scripture Text: Job 1:6–8

Focus: Suffering

When we suffer, the main question in our mind is, *why?* Rather than focusing on the problem, our primary task is to seek to understand that the wisdom of God often uses adversities to help us know that when it comes to the potential that God has in each of us, we are simply one of a kind.

Job was a real person. He was mentioned by Ezekiel (14:14) and James (5:11). Job was a Gentile. Gentiles were considered outsiders when compared to the famous children of Israel. They were thought to be descendants of Abraham's brother, Nahor. Job came to know God by the name of El Shaddai (God who is more than enough). There are more than thirty references to El Shaddai in the book of Job alone.

Job's victory was not that he had a close encounter with death. It was through his suffering that he had a closer encounter with God. He was declared by God himself to have three things going for him:

1.  He was perfect. He was mature inwardly to not be swayed by sudden and harsh events in life. He was steadfast and unmovable.

2.  He was an upright man. He had his priorities straight. Neither his wealth, children, nor his health were ever ahead of God.

3.  He eschewed (shunned) evil.

Job was the consummate Psalm 1 man.

> Blessed is the man that walketh not in the counsel of the ungodly, nor standeth in the way of sinners, nor sitteth in the seat of the scornful. But his delight is in the law of the Lord; and in his law doth he meditate day and night. And he shall be like a tree planted by the rivers of water that bringeth forth his fruit in his season; his leaf also shall not wither; and whatsoever he doeth shall prosper.
>
> Psalm 1:1 (KJV)

Here is Job. He is one of a kind. He was not tried because of his unrighteousness; his trial only established what he already was in the sight of God. It gave him a deeper insight to his relationship with God. His trial was to grant him a deeper understanding of his own nature.

The focus of the narrative of Job is that Satan wanted to prove him a sinner and God unworthy of praise and devotion. Of course, he was a liar on both counts. God's goal was to establish the sincerity of Job's faith. God does not allow trials to see if we will fail. He allows trials to strengthen our faith. Therefore, we have this story of Job. It is a picture of a righteous man suffering because God allowed it. Through this account of devotion, we see revealed the matchless wisdom of God. What seems to be a painful riddle in the human experience actually illustrates that God has uniquely made us all and that we are one of a kind. God knows you are unique. Do you know it?

The story of Job is designed to not let you stray too far away from the basic truth that both saved and unsaved people suffer. Both have problems in life. They both experience loss. They both prosper. Nonetheless, God wants both groups to know what he already knows about them.

In times of turmoil and trouble, what anchors you from being blown away? What or who sustains you in such times? Job held on to his integrity. He remained who he said he was before trouble came his way. Can you learn from Job? Can we learn that, in spite of circumstances, we must trust God and put him first?

Trust him even when you do not understand what all of his purposes are at that time.

It is important for those who have not accepted the Lord into their lives that the end of suffering is not dependent upon how badly you need it to be over. It does not matter how sincere you were when you promised God all of that stuff that you did not really intend on doing. More important than that is your willingness to surrender your life to a magnificent discovery. When you surrender your life and will to God, you will discover that there is an unrealized greatness in you. God has marvelous things in store for the rest of your life. Yes, you are indeed one of a kind.

There is no one else on the face of this earth like you. You may search and search, but you will not find anyone who is exactly like you. You are unique. You are unusual. You are you. However, it is not what you are now that is so valuable. Job had fears and shortcomings. So do all of us in one way or another. Job lived with the fear that the catastrophe that happened would someday occur. In his sorrow, he began to grieve over the day he was born. He regretted being born (Job 3:3, 11, 25). He became negative before he really knew God.

Similar to Job, all of us have to learn in life that painful riddles of human life are capable of victorious solutions. We learn that the sufferings of the righteous are not necessarily due to their own sins. We must learn that inequalities of this life are to be revisited in the life to come. We also must learn that justice will be done somehow, sometime, somewhere, and in some way.

It is not what you are that matters as much as what God wants you to be. In discussing the mercies of God, Paul described our position in this manner:

> I beseech you therefore, brethren, by the mercies of God, that ye present your bodies a living sacrifice, holy, acceptable unto God, which is your reasonable service. And be not conformed to this world: but be ye transformed by the renewing of your mind, that ye may prove what is that good, and acceptable, and perfect, will of God.
>
> Romans 12:1–2 (KJV)

The enemy of God tempts you to cause you to look around at the blessings of others and bemoan the fact that your prayers seem to go unanswered. Then he wants to convince you that perhaps it is too late now. There are too many people who have erred in their ways and spend most of their time looking over their shoulders, emotionally and spiritually crushed because they did not give their lives to Christ a long time ago, and just maybe it is too late now.

You may have missed it yesterday. You blew it the time before that, but today, when you hear his voice, harden not your heart. In other words, all the Lord desires is room in your heart. Allow his grace to be sufficient for you.

The story of Job teaches us several lessons. First, we must remember that God is sovereign. We cannot understand his workings by rational thinking alone. Our faith must find assurance in God's love and our knowledge of him. The more you love him and trust him, the easier it is to accept that whatever he does is good and righteous.

Secondly, we learn the lesson that our lives and the faith that comes from them have a direct relationship to our understanding of the character and workings of God. We understand that God's will toward us is always good and that he cares. He communicates his caring to his children (as he did to Job). This gives a fresh perspective to the God-and-man relationship.

We also learn the lesson that the struggle of faith is a personal one. There will be times when we learn that we must stand alone. Do not despair. Though we stand alone, we are not without his Spirit to walk beside us. Suffering is a solo act, but is done by your will. You must choose to suffer. That is correct. It is an act of the will. Situations that include suffering may not be your choice, but you have to choose to go through it. Choose to not only go through but also choose to grow through. Whatever you go through, you can also grow through it if you choose to do so.

You are a marked man or woman. God picked you out and preapproved you for great things. Regardless of the present conditions, you are one of a kind. Peter had a few things to say to you:

> Humble yourselves therefore under the mighty hand of God, that he may exalt you in due time: Casting all your care upon him; for he careth for you. Be sober, be vigilant; because your adversary the devil, as a roaring lion, walketh about, seeking whom he may devour: Whom resist steadfast in the faith, knowing that the same afflictions are accomplished in your brethren that are in the world. But the God of all grace, who hath called us unto his eternal glory by Christ Jesus, after that ye have suffered a while, make you perfect, strengthen, settle you.
>
> 1 Peter 5:6

Isn't it amazing how much confidence God has in you? Maybe you did not realize it before, but he wants you to know that he trusts you with life. Will you become what and who God wants you to become? It is not who you are but whose you are. It is also a matter of why you are whose you are. Only God knows the full answer. Trust me. He knows you.

Jesus Christ is one of a kind. He was born with a mission. Herod searched high and low for him that night he was born. The orders were given to slaughter all the males less than two years of age. While the massacre was in progress, Jesus was safely tucked in a manger.

As a young preteen, Jesus traveled to Jerusalem with his family. On their way back home, they discovered they were missing a son. He was lost for three days, or so they thought. They found him talking with the learned men of that day. When his earthly parents questioned him about his behavior, he told them that, "I must be about my Father's business." He was not speaking of the carpentry trade, but his heavenly Father's business of reconciling man to God.

Later, John the Baptist saw him coming down to the Jordan River to be baptized. He let us know that, "Here comes one mightier than I after me, the latchet of whose shoes I am noteworthy to stoop down and unloose," because he is one of a kind.

Finally, after healing the sick, feeding the hungry, and raising the dead, we see this unique man of God in a situation much worse than we ever could imagine. He is hanging on a cruel, rugged cross between two thieves. One ridiculed him. The other trusted him. One of the guards looked up and saw his uniqueness, and said, "Surely this must be the Son of God." But he stayed there because there is none other name under heaven given among men whereby we must be saved. He is Alpha and Omega. He is the beginning and the end. He is water in dry places and bread in a starving land. He indeed is one of a kind.

# OVERWHELMED BUT NOT OVERCOME

Scripture Text: Psalm 130:1

Focus: Spiritual Oppression and Faith

Life may present situations that are absolutely overwhelming. There is no other way to describe them. However, they do not have to overcome us. Do not become overcome by what overwhelms you. You may not have the answers, but wait on the Lord and be of good courage.

This text is a psalm of assurance. The one thing that the devil certainly does not want you to have is assurance from the Lord. He always wants to keep you guessing and wondering if God can do what he said he could do. When you get past that hurdle, then he wants you to wonder if God will do what he said he can and will do. This is especially true if you have not accepted Christ in your life.

In this psalm, we hear the voice of reality. The psalmist is expressing an all-out attack of the enemy on his spirit. He realizes that this is not the time to pretend that he knows God. This is too serious to pretend that all is well when it is not. His cry is that of a sinner who needs to be saved. In addition, yes, Jesus still saves. He saves from sin, and he saves from the depths of the despair of the child of God.

Therefore, this could also be the cry of one who feels abandoned and left to die. Like Joseph, those who called themselves brothers could have sold him out. Nevertheless, he realizes that there is only one source of help. He must look to God, regardless of the outcome. Even when you have surrendered your life to Christ, you must realize the war is just beginning. You may find yourself experiencing a literal hell on earth emotionally, financially, spiritually, and socially, and any other way.

Listen to this prayer again. "Out of the depths I cried unto Thee, O Lord…" Who would write such a psalm? History suggests it may have been Hezekiah. He was sick unto death, and the Lord delivered him out of the depths of his sickness. Until this day, the question is unsettled. Most records speak of an anonymous writer. In fact, that is not the most important factor at this time. It sounds like any of us at one time or another. However, it had to be someone with a vivid experience of desperation. Perhaps it was someone who had much over which to despair.

What is the absolute worse thing that could happen to you? Think about it. Is it losing your health? Is it losing your job or career? Is it losing a loved one, or is it your home or your car? No, the worst that could happen is that you leave this world without your sins being forgiven. That is literally what this psalm is about.

How far do you have to go before you realize you need help? How low do you have to stoop before you realize you have had enough? How long do you have to keep going down the wrong road before you realize that you are lost? In the depths of despair, the psalmist cried out to God. Despair makes us feel isolated and distant from God. This is precisely when we need God the most.

What is overwhelming in your life? If it is sin, Jesus saves and forgives. Run *to* him and stop running *from* him. Are you overwhelmed with multiple issues? Perhaps it is guilt, anger, sorrow, and/or loneliness. That which is overwhelming has met resistance to change. Since you will not go through more than you are able, what is the problem? Are you willing to change what you are doing with that which is overwhelming?

Overwhelming situations act as though it were a heavy weight pressed upon you. Paul said, "We are troubled on every side" (2 Corinthians 4:8 KJV). One interpretation is that trouble presses in on us. Trouble is a condition of distress and anxiety through real or perceived danger or the threat of danger. It is the source of worry or concern. Trouble is agitating and disturbing. Therefore, we sense pressure due to the trouble. The pressure is designed to force you away from it. Run away and hide. No one really cares anyway. At least that is what the enemy wants you to believe.

## Out of the Depths I Cried!

Where is that? The cry of the troubled often comes from deep places. There are different levels of trouble. What is mild for one may be severe for another person. In other words, some people are in trouble. Others are really in trouble. The irony of the pit is, the longer you stay in it, the deeper it gets. The danger is that a situation that is a pit today can be a grave tomorrow. A pit is just a grave without a covering. You see, what you are buried in may, in turn, bury you with it.

There are at least five companions in the pit with you. First, there is silence. You and God may only know your entry into the pit. No one else may know that you are there. No one saw you fall. No one went in with you. Words of encouragement are silenced. Hope is hushed and joy is muted in the pit. The pit is designed to quiet your praise and focus on you and your problems.

Secondly, darkness dominates the pit. There is no light in the pit. You can't see anyone but you. Your imagination can go absolutely wild in the pit. Paul gave us some help with this one: "Casting down imaginations, and every high thing that exalteth itself against the knowledge of God, and bringing into captivity every thought to the obedience of Christ," (2 Corinthians 10:5, KJV). Notice that this verse did not say the Lord will cast down your imaginations, but you must cast them down. Get them away from you. You do that by renewing your mind with imaginations that are positive and life building. The advice of Paul is recorded in Philippians 4:8 (KJV):

> Finally, brethren, whatsoever things are true, whatsoever things are honest, whatsoever things are just, whatsoever things are pure, whatsoever things are lovely, whatsoever things are of good report; if there be any virtue, and if there be any praise, think on these things.

He also said that there is a transformation process that will result in the renewing of your mind that will result in evidence of that which is good acceptable and completely the will of God for your life (Romans 12:2).

Thirdly, there is a destructive spirit in the pit. Often, is it self-destructive. With silence and no light, the strengths you used to have are torn down by anger, hopelessness, and fear. With these three, you start shutting out all meaningful help. Even when you ask for advice or help, the atmosphere of the pit will not allow you to hear or accept what you need. What you must hear is the voice of faith. Faith comes by hearing, and hearing by the Word of God. Even in the pit, the Lord hears you. The psalmist said after he cried, the Lord heard him and lifted him up from the pit.

When the Lord raises you up, notice what the psalmist describes as the "miry clay." This represents the final two companions of the pit: dust and corruption. The dust of the pit still clings to you. The dust of past failures and disappointments cling to your heart and spirit like soot from an unclean chimney. This is a picture of a saved, born-again individual with unresolved issues. Even when you are out of the pit, these issues can still be as corruptive as when you were at your lowest. The danger here is that the good you do is often corrupted by the unresolved and unhealed pain in your spirit.

Your joy is seasonal. You go back and forth between fruitful seasons and dry seasons. You try to stay busy to mask the pain, but it is still there. You are born-again but living beneath your privilege as a child of God. There is one part of the process of deliverance missing. *You* have to bring into captivity all of your thoughts to the obedience of Christ. Those evil reasonings are destroyed.

The mind itself, being overcome and taken captive, lays down all authority of its own and entirely gives itself up to perform, for the time to come, to Christ, its conqueror, the obedience of faith. In other words, you have to take back the authority over your mind. To do that, every contrary thought must become your prisoner. Arrest that thought in the name of Jesus. When thoughts are arrested, they cease all activity. Arrest those thoughts of who did something undesired or who did not do what you expected. Capture them and lock them away. You may have to arrest them on a daily basis until they stop trying to escape back into your mind and spirit. Be sure you do this in the name of Jesus Christ. Remember this: no matter how deep your pit may be, the Lord wants you to know that it is time to get out of the pit.

## I am an Overcomer!

There are two types of people in this world. There are the overcome and the overcomers. The overcome have been defeated and overtaken by people and situations. They are defeated in mind and spirit. However, in the family of God, there are the overcomers. Both experience the same kinds of dilemmas. Both have overwhelming situations with which to deal. Both face the possibility of destruction. The difference is those who overcome overwhelming situations do so by their faith in Jesus Christ.

In the book of 1 John, the writer speaks of *who-soever* is born of God nine times. However, in chapter five, he switches to the term *whatsoever* is born of God. It is not only important to know *whom* you are in Christ but also *what* you are. John is emphasizing that when Jesus Christ guides your faith and life, it is important to know what you are to do. He says what you are to do is overcome things before they overcome you. Therefore, he says, "Whatsoever is born of God overcomes the world, and this is the victory that overcomes the world, even our faith" (1 John 5:4).

An old song says that "If anybody asks you who I am, tell them I am a child of God." Allow me to amend that language to say, "If anybody asks you what I am, tell them I am an overcomer. Overcoming things is what I do. When trouble comes my way, I overcome trouble by faith and through the Word of God."

There is a divine purpose to this process. It is not to glorify ourselves but to glorify God. In the eternal wisdom of God, there is a unique means of God glorifying himself through us in spite of our fears or inadequacies. Sometimes we devalue what God values. Listen to the logic of God through Paul: "But we have this treasure in earthen vessels, that the excellency of the power may be of God, and not of us," (2

Corinthians 4:7). The excellency of the power refers to the honor that comes with overcoming. God gets the honor, and we get the victory.

That makes the power and authority excellent or unsurpassable. In days of the early church, people did not have safe deposit boxes or safes or even alarm systems. Their means of protecting valuables from thieves who came to steal was to place their most valuable possessions in the most unlikely containers. They would use the most simple earthen pots or vessels to hide their valuables. They would be safe because no one would suspect that to be the place honored with treasures of the family.

The psalmist seemed to have insight into the process of overcoming. He wrote in Psalm 130:5, "I wait for the Lord…" In fact, he said, "My soul doth wait." Until morning comes, one must utilize the God-given process of waiting. No one can stay busy enough to overcome in the physical realm. He said my soul waits. I must develop my mind, will, and emotions until my deliverance is complete. I must be careful about what I allow to infiltrate my mind. What gets in my mind will get in my spirit and eventually in my behavior. To wait with my mind, will, and emotions, one must allow a renewing of the mind through the words of faith in the Word of God. Paul wrote, "Whatsoever things are good, lovely and of a good report, to think on these things." Spend some time cultivating your mind, and your faith will increase.

As I cultivate my mind, I must also surrender my will. My will is just that—*my* will. I must learn to make some choices that will improve my situation and lead to my healing. Waiting, therefore, is a choice. It is a choice of positive action. While I wait, I must be in a mode of expectation. Why wait on the bus if it is not coming? However, the sign on the post at the bus stop says that the bus will be here at two o'clock. Therefore, my waiting is by choice based on what the sign said. God is faithful and cannot lie. The sign (Bible) said so; therefore, I will wait.

I will wait with the right attitude. The psalmist said, "I will wait more than they that wait on the morning." Sunrise is a highly emotional event. It is beautiful and exciting. Sunrise has a history of consistency. Therefore, I am assured that my waiting is not in vain.

# THE OTHER SIDE
# OF THE WALL

Scripture Text: Ephesians 2:13–18

Focus: Barriers to Faith

Around every corner of life, there seems to be another wall. Walls are Satan's attempts to block our view of what God has prepared for us. We must understand both the purpose of the wall and the victory that awaits us on the other side.

The concept of the wall is introduced in the scripture text Ephesians 2:13–18.

> But now in Christ Jesus ye who sometimes were far off are made nigh by the blood of Christ. For he is our peace, who hath made both one, and hath broken down the middle wall of partition between us; Having abolished in his flesh the enmity, even the law of commandments contained in ordinances; for to make in himself of

twain one new man, so making peace; And that he might reconcile both unto God in one body by the cross, having slain the enmity thereby: And came and preached peace to you which were afar off, and to them that were nigh. For through him we both have access by one Spirit unto the Father.

In the above scriptures, we denote a change in the way things had always been done. It is referred to as tradition. The tradition was that Gentiles (non-Jews) existed behind the wall of rejection. The phrase, "afar off…" is derived from the custom of speaking among the Hebrews. God resided in the temple according to Jewish teaching. It was a privilege to be near the temple. Those who were far away from Jerusalem and the temple were regarded as far off from God and therefore wicked and behind the wall of forgiveness and cut off from redemption.

There was only one way for the Gentiles to have the kind of access to God that they needed. The wall had to come down. That came through the love of God, whom verse four describes as rich in mercy.

The wall is described in verse 14: "For he is our peace, who hath made both one, and hath broken down the middle wall of partition between us." This is a reference to the wall that divided the inner court of the temple, open only to the Jews. Gentile visitors were only admitted to the outer court. Along the outer wall were inscriptions in both Greek and Latin. In 1871, the Greek writings were discovered to read, "No man of another race is to proceed within the partition and enclosing wall about the sanctuary: and anyone arrested there will have himself to blame for the penalty of death." Now peace with all men and peace with God is possible, because Christ allowed them and us access beyond the wall.

There are several ways of describing the wall in the English language. A wall is a partition that divides or defines the area. One area may be a bedroom and the next one a kitchen. The presence of the wall makes the difference. A wall is also a structure designed to hold back, as in the case of a retaining wall. Its very presence speaks of forbidding that which is undesirable. The concept of wall is used as an expression of a desperate situation. When one says one's back is against the wall, anyone who has experienced difficulties can identify with the idea expressed.

Additionally, runners and cyclists describe the wall as that point of extreme fatigue. Physically, one feels like giving up. Mentally, one focuses on the prize for the winner. There is no prize for those who quit. Therefore, the determined learn to focus on the invisible. They focus on the other side of the wall.

On the other side of the wall is our blessing. The wall might block our view of what God wants for us, but it cannot stop our access to the blessings of God.

Too many people allow the walls of life to block access to the treasure of God. Our heavenly Father wants grace and freedom for the sinner and abundant life for the believer. Jesus took care of that wall when he rose from the grave. There is no excuse for not going beyond the barriers Satan set up.

However, in this life we face walls of rejection, unforgiveness, discrimination, bondage, and many more. Rejection speaks of one person's disapproval of another. We expect that kind of behavior from those who have the authority. If a potential employer rejects your application that is certainly his privilege as a business owner or manager. At the same time, it does not reduce the worth or value of the applicant. But what does that have to do with the rejected person's value or worth? If your neighbor does not like you for any reason, that is his or her privilege, but that does not reduce your worth as a person. Do not give anyone the authority to reduce your sense of value because of rejection.

Another wall is unforgiveness. It is self-constructed and it must come down. The other side of the wall of unforgiveness is the blessing of peace and strength. God also promised that if you will forgive others he will forgive you. If you do not forgive, you will not be forgiven (Matthew 6:14–15). Christ died and rose that we might have the victory that is on the other side of the wall. The wall is torn down, and we can walk boldly (with confidence) to the throne of grace and find the rest (satisfaction and peace) that we need.

How do we get the wall to come down? How do we access the promises of God? Here is the secret. It is simple—so simple that even when you read it the enemy will have you doubt its validity. It is recorded in 2 Corinthians 10:3–5 (KJV):

> For though we walk in the flesh, we do not war after the flesh: (For the weapons of our warfare are not carnal, but mighty through God to the pulling down of strong holds.) Casting down imaginations, and every high thing that exalteth itself against the knowledge of God, and bringing into captivity every thought to the obedience of Christ.

Your weapon is the Word of God (the Sword of the Spirit, Ephesians 6:17b, KJV). Use it in your prayer life. Use it in your time of meditation. Speak it to yourself and your situation. Focus on the other side of the wall. The Bible declares that the just (righteous) live by faith. It also says in the text that God is our peace, the peace of God that passes all understanding. The peace that originates with God is available to all who have made peace with God. Peace breaks down the wall of hatred, discrimination, and confusion. The writer of Proverbs penned, "A soft answer turns away wrath..." It is also recorded that he will keep him in perfect peace whose mind is stayed on him because he trusts in him.

Jesus added to the topic when he left us a legacy of peace: "Peace I leave with you, my peace I give unto you: not as the world giveth, give I unto you. Let not your heart be troubled, neither let it be afraid" (John 14:27, NIV). When you stand on the Word of God, there is no such thing as intimidation from the devil or anybody else.

When you look past the distractions and hindrances of the enemy, you will find freedom from fear and anxiety. Paul wrote to the saints at Philippi and challenged them to use praise as a means of getting to the other side of the wall (Philippians 4:4). Praise your way to the other side. Then he said to relax and let your gentleness be displayed. Let the peace of God saturate your mind, body, and spirit by meditating on the Word of God. Next, he advised to not allow you to be anxious for any reason. Anxieties are distractions and preoccupation with things causing stress and pressure. Jesus said simply to throw (cast) them on him because he cares and keeps on caring for you. When you go through this process, you find a miracle. The peace that passes all understanding will keep (stand guard over) your hearts and minds through Christ Jesus. The enemy will no longer be able to invade your heart and mind. Praise God!

In the book of Hebrews we find a roll call of those who, by faith, looked beyond the walls in their way. Abraham trusted God, and it was accounted to him for righteousness (Galatians 3:6, KJV). Moses conquered the wall of the Red Sea. By faith, the walls of Jericho fell down flat. All of these and more had their share of victory. They all received a good report through faith but did not receive the promise that we have. They were not able to see the Lord, Jesus Christ. God has provided a better experience for us who have received Christ.

To get beyond the wall, Jesus said that you have the authority to speak to the wall (mountain): "For verily I say unto you, That whosoever shall say unto this mountain, Be thou removed, and be thou cast into the sea; and shall not doubt in his heart, but shall believe that those things which he saith shall come to pass; he shall have whatsoever he saith," (Mark 11:23, KJV). Stop looking at the wall, and speak the Word of God to it and it shall be removed. The Word of God is the authority of God over any situation. When your prayer includes the words that God has already said, two powerful events take place. First, when God's word goes out it will accomplish the purpose for which it was sent. The purposes of God for you will be manifested in obedience to the sovereign will of God.

Secondly, the Word of God ignites the fires of your faith. The fuel for the fire is obedience. Faith is not simply hoping for things to get better. Faith is trust and reliance on what God has said. According to Hebrews 11:3 (KJV), through faith we understand that the worlds were framed by the word of God so that things that are seen were not made of things which do appear. The power to create whatever needs to come into your life resides in your faith. Magically? No. Creative faith is often a process of divine revelation for the children of God. Please know that God will use you in this process. In every creative miracle in the Bible, the recipient of the miracle had a part to play. A blind man was told to go wash, and others were told to take up their bed and walk. As you pray and believe, God will reveal your part of the answer. Trust God and prepare to see walls come down.

# DREAMS, TEARS, AND A SONG

Scripture Text: Psalm 137:1–4

Focus: Hope, Purpose, and Restoration

The hopes and dreams of people are often shattered by the unexpected or the undesired events of life. This is a word about the process of restoration. We have dreams that are interrupted by situations that result in tears. But praise God. He gives us a song of hope and a predetermined purpose. The words of the psalmist say it best from Psalm 40:1–3 (AMP):

> *I waited* patiently and expectantly for the Lord; and He inclined to me and heard my cry. He drew me up out of a horrible pit [a pit of tumult and of destruction], out of the miry clay (froth and slime), and set my feet upon a rock, steadying my steps and establishing my goings. And He has put a new song in my mouth, a song of praise

to our God. Many shall see and fear (revere and worship) and put their trust and confident reliance in the Lord.

Dreams are wonderful in that they often take us to places to which we can no longer travel. They take us back to our childhood with all of the innocence and carefree times. They also allow us to project ourselves into the possibilities of great tomorrows without the burdens of today. Dreams are defined as those things for which we hope and long to obtain. They include our ambitions and aspirations. The beauty of dreams is that they may also include those things that may be difficult to obtain and far removed from the present circumstances.

Such was the case when the people of the Lord were taken away captive from their own land. The experience was devastating. Many had died. Families had been separated and scattered. Those who were children were now senior citizens and had never seen the city of David. It was indeed an unhappy time. It all seems to have been a long, bad dream. The grief, sorrow, and humiliation would be forever etched in their minds. They had been saved by the goodness of God but could never forget the humiliation of defeat. They could not erase the hardships of the long journey. They would never forget the years of being homesick.

When we read the chronicle of their experience, we hear the loneliness and agony of their loss. "By the rivers of Babylon, there we [captives] sat down, yes, we wept when we [earnestly] remembered Zion [the city of our God imprinted on our hearts]" (Psalm 137:1). In their captivity, the view of a free-flowing river caused dreams to come alive in their minds. Daydreaming can be more powerful than dreams in the night. One is in control of dreams in the day. They took a position of grief. They stooped down in a position of the mourners. They wept. The good of it was that they remembered. They recalled the joy and peace of home. You must have a visual image of what you desire before you can move toward it. Somewhere in the world of the Internet came a story about a prisoner of war (POW) in the Vietnam war who survived by daily practicing golf shots in his mind to protect his sanity. It is said that when he was released or rescued, he returned home. When he resumed his favorite activity of golf, he became a champion player. He did not let captivity steal his dream.

No matter what is happening or what has happened, we cannot allow anything to steal our dreams. Our dreams provide motivation for the underlying purpose of God in our lives. Dreams give birth to vision. When we recall the former years, it allows us to compare yesterday with today. This leads to projecting how to improve the present situation tomorrow. There are plenty of dream stealers in the land. Often, they are disguised as well-meaning relatives and friends who want to caution you to "hope for the best but expect the worst." What a ridiculous mindset! How can one be motivated by expecting what is not desired?

Don't listen to them. Do not allow present conditions to vaporize your dreams. Dreams often contain our suppressed desires. Desire is the primary ingredient for faith. Faith is the substance of things hoped for [desired] and the evidence of that which have not yet seen. The Amplified uses the following language: "*Now faith* is the assurance (the confirmation, the title deed) of the things [we] hope for, being the proof of things [we] do not see and the conviction of their reality [faith perceiving as real fact what is not revealed to the senses]," (Hebrews 11:1). Faith does not ignore reality but provides us the fuel to move forward in spite of the limitations and obstacles in the way.

On the other hand, dreams can be the place of regret for the things we wish we could undo in our past. This leads to songs of remorse and hopelessness. The tragedy of the attitude of the children of Israel was that not only did they stoop down in a mourning position, but they gave up their instruments of praise. Hear them now in the Amplified version:

On the willow trees in the midst of [Babylon]
we hung our harps. For there they who led us

captive required of us a song with words, and our tormentors and they who wasted us required of us mirth, saying, "Sing us one of the songs of Zion." How shall we sing the Lord's song in a strange land?

Psalm 137:2–4

The obvious lesson here is to never give up your harp. The harp is the instrument of praise. It is symbolic of the instrument of your voice. Again, from Psalm 40, the writer emphasizes that when he was raised from a horrible pit [the place of bondage] and the miry clay [clinging circumstances], God put a new song in his mouth. It is a song of redemption and hope and praise to Almighty God.

## The Ministry of Tears

Until morning comes, we must also understand the ministry of tears. This psalm was probably written toward the end of the Babylonian captivity. Their enemies had carried the Jews captive from their own land. To complete their woes, they insulted them; they required of them entertainment and a song. This was very barbarous—also profane—for no songs would serve but the songs of Zion. The very thought of honoring such a request brought great sorrow. The real issue was that they were not requesting an ordinary song but one of the songs that belong to the praises of God! Those were the songs that brought back memories of the power, majesty, and loving nature of God back home. Now all seems lost to never sing songs like that again. So they sat down and wept. With their harps dangling gently from the willow tree limbs, they wept.

In the mind of this writer, just perhaps the tears served an additional purpose. There are many purposes for tears. Were these tears of sorrow, depression, or grief? Perhaps they were tears of faith. Tears in Scripture play a unique role in spiritual breakthrough. This text, along with several others regarding a spirit of brokenness, pictures a variety of purposes and functions related to tears.

No mistake about it; there are tears of sorrow. The Lord told the prophet to turn around and give the prophet this message: "Go back and say to Hezekiah, leader of my people, 'This is what the Lord God of your ancestor David says: "I've heard your prayer. *I've seen your tears.* Now I'm going to heal you. The day after tomorrow you will go to the Lord's temple""[3]. I have seen your tears. God is aware of all the activities of the soul. The Lord recognizes your sorrow. He will hear you for more than your tears. He will hear you because of what he sees in you. He will hear you for your purpose and destiny.

There are also tears of joy. When Esau ran out to meet his brother, Jacob, he embraced and kissed him.

Then the Bible records that they wept. The joy of restoration was an outgrowth of their tears. Their years of separation had become a burden to both of them for their own reasons. Jacob feared Esau, and Esau had to live with the guilt of gluttony and disregard for his birthright. Their tears had to break through their years of stubbornness. Tears were the catalyst for restoration.

Then there are tears of compassion. The greatest example is Christ himself in John 11:35: "Jesus wept." Those who observed his compassion connected his tears with his love for his friend: "See how He loved him." However, it seems as if the love of Jesus was for more than Lazarus. Certainly, he could have spoken the word where he was, and Lazarus would be raised from the dead instantly. He demonstrated that with the sick daughter of Jabirus. Christ purposely delayed answering the visitation request of the sister of his friend for four days. He did so to give God the glory and minister to those who would see a resurrected Lazarus. His compassion was far-reaching. You cannot have real ministry without compassion.

There are tears of desperation, worry, and extreme anxiety. In the book of Esther, Mordecai wept bitterly when he discovered the plot of Haman to have all of the Jews killed. His desperation spread to every part of the country. Desperation comes when it seems we have nowhere to turn. The psalmist experienced the same dilemma in Psalm 42:3, 5 (KJV):

> My tears have been my meat day and night, while they continually say unto me, "Where is thy God?" He then began to question himself, "Why art thou cast down, O my soul?" and "why art thou disquieted in me?" Hope thou in God: for I shall yet praise him for the help of his countenance.

In times of desperation, trust God and turn to him.

Tears of travail represent the experience of every mother who has given birth through the pains of labor and travail. It is the agony of delivery. The period of travail may be long or short in duration. To the one in labor, it may seem like an eternity. The purpose of labor makes it worth the effort and struggle. The birth of the baby brings great joy. God wants you to give birth to great victory, but labor comes first. The writer of Hebrews reminds us, "There remaineth therefore a rest to the people of God. Let us labour therefore to enter into that rest, lest any man fall after the same example of unbelief," (Hebrews 4:9, 11, KJV). Great deliverance awaits those who are willing to go through great tribulations. But remember, we are more than conquerors through Christ who loves us.

Finally, there are tears of repentance. These are the most important tears we will shed in our lives. Tears of repentance must be distinguished from tears of guilt. One can shed tears over a regretted behavior but never change behaviors through repentance. Tears of repentance represent regret over having offended our heavenly Father. A broken spirit and a contrite (remorseful) heart represent the true passion that accompanies repentance. When true repentance takes place, a change will be manifest (a new creature will emerge in terms of lifestyle).

In another liturgical hymn, the psalmist gave additional insight into the meaning and power of tears. Psalm number 126 was probably composed by Ezra, at the return of Israel from Babylon. Those who are returned were called upon to be thankful; those who still remained there were prayed for and encouraged. Here is the message:

> *When the* Lord brought back the captives [who returned] to Zion, we were like those who dream [it seemed so unreal]. They who sow in tears shall reap in joy and singing. He who goes forth bearing seed and weeping [at needing his precious supply of grain for sowing] shall doubtless come again with rejoicing, bringing his sheaves with him.
>
> Psalm 126:1, 5–6 (AMP)

Now pay close attention to verses five and six: "They who sow [plant seeds of] tears shall reap [have a harvest] of joy and praise." You plant during the planting season. The planting of tears will be during the dry seasons in your life. Tears represent that seemingly endless period between the dream and the song. Tears represent the individuality of a traumatic experience. No one can shed your tears for you. They are evidence of your involvement, whether directly or indirectly. Tears precede deliverance.

Unfortunately, many people try to suppress tears. Society has associated tears with weakness. To the contrary, anyone strong enough to be real with his or her emotions is on the road to deliverance. Emotional barriers of fear and hopelessness can be torn down when they are faced with the power of faith. However, deliverance is more than an event. It is a process. Tears become the outlet for the soul. They become evidence of the intensity of the situation. Yes, weeping only came for the night, and joy is arriving with the morning. By divine inspiration, I believe that your joy brings the morning. Morning is ushered in from the depths of the praises of the soul. It becomes a testimony to all who have witnessed your sorrow. The psalmist continues in Psalm 126:2–4 (AMP):

> Then were our mouths filled with laughter, and
> our tongues with singing. Then they said among

the nations, "The Lord has done great things for them." The Lord has done great things for us! We are glad! Turn to freedom our captivity and restore our fortunes, O Lord, as the streams in the South (the Negev) [are restored by the torrents].

Your deliverance will not be a secret. God will reward you openly!

## Lord, Give Me a Song!

After the reflections of dreams and the cleansing of the spirit with tears, you must release a song. Neither the quality nor the lyrics are as important as the type of song. Do not sing a song of grief but a song of hope, a song of faith, a song of praise.

God designed you for praise. You were made in his image and likeness. God has angels around him throughout eternity, releasing praise. It has been said that the clapping of hands by the saints is similar to the fluttering of the wings of angels as they fly and praise God. No wonder the writer encouraged us to "clap your hands all ye people; shout unto God with the voice of triumph" (Psalm 47:1). Praise intimidates the devil. It becomes our weapon of offence to accompany the sword of the Spirit (which is the Word of God).

One of the most powerful scriptures in the Bible challenges us to live a life of praise. "In every thing give thanks: for this is the will of God in Christ Jesus concerning you," (1 Thessalonians 5:18, KJV). Jesus taught us to pray the will of the Father to be done in the earth as it is in heaven. Therefore, our daily prayer should be, "God, give me a song." A song is a declaration of confidence and a threat to the enemy of God. Since God inhabits the praises of his people, our song invites the presence of God to be manifest in our lives.

The power of 1 Thessalonians 5:18a is in the phrase "in everything give thanks..." In every situation, look for the good to give God praise until morning comes. No, every situation is not a praise situation, but God is no less worthy of the praise.

The exciting news is that praise is not limited to the singing of songs to music. Praise is also manifest in our lifestyle. The highest praise is more than the words "halleluiah" but in our obedience to God. In other words, in every situation, no matter how difficult, obey God. When faced with loneliness and mood shifts to depression, obey God. Obey him with service to others and to yourself. Take care of yourself. Watch your health and eating habits. Strengthen the physical and spiritual man. Pray the prayer of Psalm 19:14: "Let the words of my mouth, and the meditation of my heart, be acceptable in thy sight, O Lord, my strength, and my redeemer." Watch what you say and speak into your life. Let it be positive, and make certain it gives God the glory.

# THE GIFT OF TIME

Scripture Text: Revelation 14:13–15

Background Text: Ephesians 5:15–16

Focus: The Value of Time

This chapter seeks to establish the importance of time with the sinner and the saint. The sinner must not regret the loss of time due to past mistakes. The saint must appreciate time and redeem it. In either case, time is a gift that only God can give.

I remember when I was ten years old in Mrs. Davis's fifth grade class at Dunbar Elementary School, Muskogee, Oklahoma. I remember calculating (with pencil and paper), at her direction, how old I would be when the year 2000 came. All of us, including me, could not comprehend the reality of such an event. At the turn of the century, some forty-three years later, facing the reality of that calculation, it brings reality to my doorstep. The day is coming when we will no longer exist here on earth. One day, we all will be gone, and we will be gone forever.

Believers know this. This is the reason we are willing to separate ourselves from the world and live for Christ. It is the reason we are willing to give all to Christ and his mission. It is the reason believers do not live in sin but, by the power of God, learn to conquer the sins and temptations of this life. This is the reason we refuse to deny Christ. It is the reason we suffer the persecutions of this world, the ridicule, the abuse, mockery, strange looks, sneers, isolation, cursing, and sometimes imprisonment and death. Therefore, we have given our lives to Jesus Christ. Jesus Christ is the only one who can free us from sin and make us acceptable to God. He has given us the right to live forever.

In the meantime, what do we do about today? Do we spend our time moaning over mistakes and failures? Do we grieve over losses as if there is no hope of restoration? Absolutely not! We must turn our attention to what we have left and not be halted by what or whom we have lost.

The profoundly wise and knowledgeable preacher declared in Ecclesiastes chapter three, "To every thing there is a season, and a time to every purpose under the heaven." The teacher shows that we are subject to times and changes over which we have little or no control and contrasts this state with God's eternity and sovereignty. God's sovereignty predetermines all of life's activities. What we have left is certainly obvious in the above reference. Time is something we all have in common. No one has too little, and no one has too much. We all have twenty-four hours—no more and no less. It is not how much time you have left but what you do with it. Time is divinely appointed.

Psalm 31:15a (KJV): "My times are in thy hand." This is a reference to the future of the writer. Each day is one gift at a time. Only the Lord knows the extent of that time. What is our responsibility? It is to value each day and provide a legacy for those who follow. The future is not ours to worry over. The wisdom of Christ is articulated in Matthew 6:34 (AMP): "So do not worry or be anxious about tomorrow, for tomorrow will have worries and anxieties of its own. Sufficient for each day is its own trouble." In other words, approach each day with value and focus. Each day is a valuable opportunity to obtain the fulfillment that Christ promised with the abundant life. If we waste time trying to manipulate tomorrow, we will miss the value of today.

The gift of time is precious. It is the gift that only God can grant. He created it for us. A gift, by definition, is that which is given which usually provides pleasure. God created man for his glory and placed him in a garden called Eden. Eden means place of delight or pleasure. God's intent was to provide a place of delight and pleasure for his creation, man, eternally.

When Adam sinned and mankind fell from the grace gifts God had granted, the gift of time became limited. Nevertheless, through the second Adam, Jesus Christ, life and time were provided all of us who believe. Jesus declared it in this manner, "The thief cometh not, but for to steal, and to kill, and to destroy: I am come that they might have life, and that they might have it more abundantly," (John 10:10, KJV). So much time is relegated to what we have lost or may be losing and not enough focus on the time we have left.

Redemption is a metaphor used in both Old and New Testaments to describe God's merciful and costly action on behalf of his people. The basic meaning of the word is release or freedom on payment of a price, deliverance by a costly method. When used of God, it does not suggest that he paid a price to anyone but rather that his mercy required his almighty power and involved the greatest possible depth of suffering. God redeemed Israel from Egypt by delivering the people from bondage and placing them in a new land.

The verb *padhah*, in its secular use, is entirely given over to express ransom-price (e.g., Leviticus 27:27, Numbers 18:15–17, Psalm 49:7). When it is used of the Lord's ransoming work, thirteen out of the thirty-nine references allude to the Exodus (e.g., Deuteronomy 9:26, 2 Samuel 7:23, Nehemiah 1:10). Three references speak specifically of the forgiveness of sins (Deuteronomy 21:8, Psalm 130:8, Isaiah 1:27)[4].

To appreciate the New Testament theme of redemption, the position of human beings as slaves of sin must be assumed (John 8:33–34). Therefore, they must be set free in order to become the liberated servants of the Lord (Mark 10:45). This redemption, paid for by the costly sacrifice of the life of Jesus, is a completed act as far as God is concerned. But the results of the redemption as far as we are concerned are experienced in part now and in full at the resurrection of the dead (Luke 21:27–28, Romans 8:23, Ephesians 4:30).

As we approach each day, we must have a strategy for successful use of the time we have to fulfill our assignment. Paul wrote to the church at Ephesus and spoke direction into their lives. The first component of the strategy is to realize where you are and make sure you are walking in the light of Jesus Christ. We cannot walk in the light or with Christ if we are asleep and inattentive to his will (Ephesians 5:14).

However, he assures us that Christ will provide the light in which to walk and live. In times of loss, we must not lose focus on the priority of a lifestyle that is pleasing to the Lord. Grief is a melancholy emotion. It is not associated with joy. Therefore, the challenge of this strategy is to remember the edict, "In every thing give thanks: for this is the will of God in Christ Jesus concerning you." The will of God can only be done through Christ Jesus. It is the will of God that you survive these trying times and enter into the joy of the Lord, which is designed to strengthen you.

The second aspect of the divine strategy is to live *circumspectly* (Ephesians 5:15–16). Circumspect living is living in wisdom. The circumspect lifestyle is one that is unwilling to act without first weighing the risks or consequences. Wisdom must be employed in every aspect of life: emotionally, socially, physically, and spiritually. Take time to laugh. The wise man, Solomon, instructs us, "A merry heart doeth good like a medicine: but a broken spirit drieth the bones," (Proverbs 17:22, KJV*).* The God's Word translation reads, "A joyful heart is good medicine, but depression drains one's strength." The challenge here is not to act happy. The challenge is to relax the mind, body, and spirit with lighter matters. Take the time to spend with children, pets, or friends who add value to life with simple things. Notice the smile of a child, the warmth of a mother's hug, or the trusting puppy with a vigorously wagging tail. The loss will never be forgotten, but the medicine of laughter will speed up the healing process.

Wisdom is also centered in noticing your own physical wellbeing. You must not neglect your body. Stressful times often lead to neglect of the one in distress. Take the time to get a medical examination. Exercise and proper eating will foster healthy recovery and allow time to heal totally. This is no time to walk foolishly. Foolishness shows a lack of good sense or judgment. The foolish get lost in the problem and literally miss the solution.

Social wisdom is a reflection of an awareness of relationships and surroundings. People often have hidden agendas. People you have known for years may have unsavory motives. Weigh decisions carefully. People you have trusted may not be as trustworthy now. This is not given to breed contempt or suspicion but a reality factor. Financial decisions are perhaps the most critical. Take the time to pray and seek the guidance of the Lord along with a trustworthy person.

The gift of time is a fleeting phenomenon. The Pauline text gives a priceless insight into its management: "Redeeming the time, because the days are evil," (Ephesians 5:16b). Redemption, as described above, is a powerful concept as it relates to time and our future. Here, it refers to taking advantage of every opportunity to maximize the time we have left. Each day is a precious gift that will become a faded memory if we do not take advantage of it. Tomorrow is not a guarantee. The Word of God directs us to focus on today: "So do not worry or be anxious about tomorrow, for tomorrow will have worries and anxieties of its own. Sufficient for each day is its own trouble," (Matthew 6:34, AMP). So what is our task for today? The classic answer is to attend to the opportunities each day provides. Sometimes the opportunities are masked by our emotions of sadness and gloom. The enemy of God would have you miss it with such distractions. What the enemy highlights as evil, God wants to show you the good.

The psalmist wrote, "This is the day which the Lord has brought about; we will rejoice and be glad in it" (Psalm 118:24, AMP). The joy of each day is the strength that it brings to fulfill your purpose. The day is brought about, provided, and ushered into your life by God himself. God wants your day to be a day of opportunity for greatness. There are no accidental blessings. Each incident is part of the plan. Of course, the enemy of God attempts to interrupt the plan with coincidences. There are many things that show up on your way to your opportunity that will seem to be ordained by God. This is not necessarily true. It is true that God wants to bless you in spite of unplanned and unforeseen circumstances. It is not, however, part of the plan of God. Coincidences often parallel incidences of blessings.

Well, how do you handle the coincidences? Look to Job for the answer. He said, "All the days of my appointed time will I wait until my change comes." Waiting for the change to come is parallel to waiting until the morning comes. The secret is the commitment to wait. Waiting is a vehicle for expectations. Waiting requires the development of an attitude of focused faith in God. The change is not an event. It is a process. It is a process planted in the garden of desire, sprinkled with hope, and nourished by faith.

The change that comes resides in you. You have to be developed as you wait with patience.

Finally, the process of waiting includes the all-important activity of transformation by renewing your mind. Paul said not to conform to this world. Conforming to the world's idea of deliverance may lead to many destructive elements, i.e. drugs, alcohol, promiscuous behavior, etc. Conformity involves behaving or thinking in a socially expected way. In other words, the world says do what everyone else is doing whether it is effective or not. The Word of God sets a different standard.

Be transformed by the renewing of your mind. Transformation is the final aspect of the process of healing. It involves what you say to yourself. It involves replacing the negative in your mind and spirit with the word of faith from the Word of God. The purpose is to prove what is the good, acceptable, and perfect will of God ([Romans] 12:1-2). The will of God is good (beneficial to you). God has plans for you. Those plans are good and not evil toward an expected end (Jeremiah 29:11). The will of God is that which is acceptable to him. Our transformation is to seek that which is acceptable on God's terms and not ours. The primary element that is acceptable to God is for us to learn to give thanks in everything—not because of everything but in the midst of everything. The will of God is perfect. It is complete and mature. Transformation leads to development of a mature spirit that enables us to endure and conquer all things.

Paul describes the best use of our gift of time in the face of all odds:

> Speaking to yourselves in psalms and hymns and spiritual songs, singing and making melody in your heart to the Lord; Giving thanks always for all things unto God and the Father in the name of our Lord Jesus Christ.
>
> Ephesians 5:19–20

# RESTING IN THE FAVOR OF GOD

Scripture Text: Genesis 6:8–12

Focus: The Favor of God

God's plan for man is not always obvious. Many will miss it. Meanwhile, chaos and destruction will seem to be the rule of the day. There is, however, the divine favor that God has provided for the deliverance of mankind from the destruction of this world. The favor of God is released through salvation and deliverance through his Son, Jesus Christ.

One of the most intriguing stories in the Bible is that of a man named Noah. It is much more than just a story about a man who built a boat and survived a flood. It is the account of a man with unusual favor from God. God's favor on the life of this obedient, courageous, and faithful servant was more valuable than money. The favor of God literally saved his life.

Almost nothing is known of the early life of Noah. The first time we see him in Scripture is when he is five hundred years old. His father seemed to be the godly man, Lamech, who gave his son a proper name, Rest. Noah, Rest, gained confidence in God and learned to rest in his word. Noah also lived in a time when men were totally corrupt.

However, he was a man of great character. It is recorded that he not only knew God but that he walked with God. He was the grandson of Methuselah, who lived 969 years and was the tenth generation from Adam. In a time of moral darkness, he was intimate with God and learned of God's plan to destroy mankind. We especially remember Noah as the man who accomplished a task given by God that seemed almost foolish and impossible.

Noah built an ark for the destruction that was coming. God gave him a difficult task with specific directions for his own deliverance. Most of the people around him neither knew that nor believed that such a thing could happen. This is what people will do, especially if they are not walking with God. They walk by sight and not by faith. Hosea declared, "My people are destroyed for the lack of knowledge," (Hosea 4:6). It was not the lack of education, nor is it today. You may be well educated and not have the knowledge that you need to survive this treacherous world.

> For as in the days that were before the flood they were eating and drinking, marrying and giving in marriage, until the day that Noah entered into the ark. And knew not until the flood came, and took them all away; so shall also the coming of the Son of man be.
>
> Matthew 24:38–39

## The Days of Noah

Noah preached one message for 120 years: "Rain is coming." How did he know what others did not? How did he stay motivated in all of that time? It was apparent that others were blind to what Noah could clearly see. The question is, what kept him going with such certainty for an event that had never happened? The answer is simple. Noah had favor with God. Favor is a special privilege that comes from a relationship with God. It is a privilege that many are not willing to pursue. It comes with a walk with God that requires one to become a living sacrifice to what he or she wants.

It was as if God stood face-to-face with Noah and spoke into his life a revelation of hope in a hopeless time. This called for focused action. He could not be distracted from his assignment. The assignment was to save his family. It was no time for business as usual. It was a time to prepare for the unseen, for the unexpected. He had to remain focused in spite of the negative conversations he endured. By faith he operated although no one, not even his family, could understand the full extent of the promise of God. Favor is escorted by faith and assured by the Word of God. One thing that Noah knew for certain was that he had a word from God.

## God Is Speaking

God is still speaking as he did in the days of Noah. God spoke to Noah, and he obeyed. He will speak to you, or he will speak through someone to you. But either way, you may rest assured that God will speak. He speaks through the events of our lives. He speaks through circumstances. Our task is to listen and obey. Even during critical times and tragic circumstances, the voice of God is available to the spiritual ear. God speaks to those with whom he has favor. He spoke to Adam in the garden of Eden. He spoke with Enoch and walked with him into eternity. God spoke to Lazarus and told him to come forth out of a dead existence. God wants to communicate with you, whatever your situation in life. Go to him in prayer. He will listen, and he will answer.

When you walk with God and he releases his favor on your behalf, a wonderful set of events begins. First, there is an unusual peace that comes with hearing from God. Paul described it as a peace that surpasses understanding (Phil 4:6–7). The God's Word version communicates this truth as follows:

> Do not fret *or* have any anxiety about anything, but in every circumstance *and* in everything, by prayer and petition (definite requests), with thanksgiving, continue to make your wants known to God.
>
> Philippians 4:6 (AMP)

This is what the devil can't quite understand or interrupt. He is a deceiver. Therefore, he sends negative thoughts and distracting ideas to your mind. It is part of the human experience. When he does, the peace of God provides a spiritual antidote through the Word of God. We receive this solid advice from the writing of Paul in 2 Corinthians 10:5 (KJV): "Casting down imaginations, and every high thing that exalteth itself against the knowledge of God, and bringing into captivity every thought to the obedience of Christ."

Secondly, the assurance of favor raises your confidence level. Let me refer to it in the terminology of the novice Christian and say that "somehow" we know what to do and say without knowing what to do or say. In better terms, it is the infusion of knowledge and wisdom that comes from the Holy Spirit. It is a gift of grace—God's grace.

# His Grace Is Sufficient

Grace: Hebrew, *hen;* Greek, *charis.* A term used by the biblical writers with a considerable variety of meaning: 1) Properly speaking, that which affords joy, pleasure, delight, charm, sweetness, loveliness; 2) good will, loving-kindness, mercy, etc.; 3) the kindness of a master toward a slave. By analogy, grace has come to signify the kindness of God to man (Luke 1:30).

The word *grace* is often used to express the concept of kindness given to someone who doesn't deserve it: hence, undeserved favor, especially that kind or degree of favor bestowed on sinners through Jesus Christ (Ephesians 2:4–5). Grace, therefore, is that unmerited favor of God toward fallen man whereby for the sake of Christ—the only begotten of the Father, full of grace and truth (John 1:14)—he has provided for man's redemption. He has, from all eternity, determined to extend favor toward all who have faith in Christ as Lord and Savior.

Grace is the medium or instrument through which God has effected the salvation of all believers (Titus 2:11). Grace is also the sustaining influence enabling the believer to persevere in the Christian life (Acts 11:23, 20:32; 2 Corinthians 9:14). It is also used as a token or proof of salvation (1:5). A special gift of grace is imparted to the humble (James 4:6; 1 Peter 5:5). Grace can also refer to the capacity for the reception of divine life (1:10). It may also mean a gift of knowledge (1 Corinthians 1:4) and thanksgiving or gratitude expressed for favor (10:30; 1 Timothy 1:1–2). No small thing, this grace. It is a favor that is sufficient. "My grace is sufficient for thee," (he told Saul).

## Jesus, the Divine Favor of God

God so loved the world He gave them a Favor
He came to reveal the plan of the Father
But He was rejected and is still being rejected today
He was despised by men and not esteemed
only as one smitten by God
But whosoever believeth on Him shall not perish but
shall have everlasting life.

God has provided a rest in his favor. It is a place of peace and satisfaction with the will of God, regardless of the circumstances we face. Learn to relax and rest in his provisions. Salvation is not only about heaven but also a provision for earth living. It is not only about the saving of our souls but the saving and deliverance of our minds, bodies, and spirits. Take your rest and enjoy the favor.

# SOMEONE WHO CARES

Scripture Text: John 8:23–28

Focus: Compassion

Compassion requires patience. Patience is only used in the context of relationships with people. Everything else is endured. This lesson will speak to the need we all have in our lives. It is a need that is often delayed or denied even by the closest relationship. However, it is a need that can by fulfilled by someone who cares.

This is the sixth of the series of "I am" statements that Jesus declared about himself. The power of what he said may seem hidden from direct view. It was embedded in how Jesus speaks as much as what he speaks. In this text, Christ already feels the cold shadows of death approaching him. However, in typical fashion, he thinks of the needs of others rather than himself. He speaks to the confused, the frustrated, and those who still need to know who he is. In summary, he said, "I am only here for a little while. After I have gone away, you may begin to seek me, but it will be too late."

Their immediate response was that maybe he was going to commit suicide. To this, Jesus explains the difference between them and him and, in turn, demonstrates his patience with mortal man. "You are from below, I am from above, you are of this world, and I am not of this world. But if you believe in me, you can rise above where you are now to where God wants you to be."

In verse twenty-four he demonstrates more patience, saying, "What I keep repeating over and over." His patience seems almost exhausted. Would it be worthwhile to try any longer to explain? Nevertheless, he repeats a message made so clear in previous "I am" statements. How often does Jesus repeat lessons of righteousness to people who forget so easily? Yet he understands and takes us where we are and leads us to where we need to go. How often is Jesus like Daddy taking his little boy or girl for a walk? Daddy's stride is long and defined. The little one keeps up for a few paces but soon has to trot to keep up. Finally exhausted, the child's strength runs out, and one of two events occur: Either Daddy shortens his pace to let the little one keep up, or the child whines and cries until he or she is finally picked up in Daddy's arms and carried the rest of the way.

Jesus, the Good Shepherd, the Open Door, the Resurrection and the Life, the Bread of Life, and the Light of the World is also someone who cares for us. When we are too slow or too weak, "He gives power to the faint; and to them that have no might he increases strength" (Isaiah 40:29, KJV). To those who stumble from one problem or one heartbreak after another, it is written that, "The steps of a good man are ordered by the Lord, and he delights in his way" (Psalm 37:23, KJV). To those who have doubts and fears, James speaks, "If any of you lack wisdom let him ask of God that gives to all men liberally and not reprimand you, and it shall be given him" (James 1:5, KJV).

The one who cares is patient and shows it. Patience may be defined as compassionate caring. Patience is faithfully tolerant. It requires forgiveness. It also requires restraint in times of frustration. It means not giving up on another. Jesus compassionately understands. He finds us out of agreement with his will, and what does he do? He waits! How amazing is that? He waits with compassion. He is from above, yet he is someone who cares.

All of us need someone who understands and has patience. Understanding requires two elements. One factor is time. The other is proximity. You cannot get to understand the ways of anyone with whom you have not invested any time. The investment of time with three types of people will be vital to your character development. You first need to invest time with people who are where you want to be, whether it is financially, spiritually, or otherwise. You need someone in your own life who can pour into you that which you lack. Secondly, you need to invest time with people at your level of development. This inner circle of associates will be important for accountability in your progress. They should be people who care enough to tell you what you *need* to hear and not what you *want* to hear.

Finally, you need someone in your life that you care enough about to pour into their life. It should be someone who is where you have been or below where you are in your development now. Yes, it is more blessed to give than to receive. The more you become the someone who cares in the life of another, the more you will begin to focus on being the best you can be, no matter what else you are facing. In any of these levels, you must be certain that your involvement is genuine. It must not simply be another of the many mundane tasks of the week to get through and erase from your calendar or laundry list of things to do. Remember, people do not care how much you know until they know who much you care.

Most of the problems people have during times of great difficulty are relationship issues. Many marriages and family wounds would heal more readily if someone cared enough to simply say, "I'm sorry. Please forgive me." The longer the wound remains unattended, the more difficult it is for it to heal. Time is an ingredient in healing but not the sole solution to healing. One must be cautious about dismissing spiritual attacks on one's spiritual life as a passing thing. Take every opportunity available to confront the enemy of your soul with the Word of God. In times of gloom and doom, the enemy of the mind will lead you to turn against those closest to you. Problems and situations long forgotten will surface when you are hurting. Remember, you are the only one responsible for your emotions. No one can ruin your day unless you allow him or her that privilege. Your feelings are just that—*your* feelings. Don't cast blame on any one else for your feelings.

I continue to find great solace in the timeless words of the psalmist in number twenty-three: "The Lord is my shepherd, I shall not want. He leads me beside the still waters, he restores my soul." The shepherd is the quintessential caregiver. The one who gives care is neither obligated nor designed to solve the problem. The wisdom of the psalmist is in recognizing the role of the shepherd from his own experience. The shepherd guides the sheep to their destination. In the process of time, provisions for food and water are made available by guiding the sheep to the best location for nourishment. Therefore, I shall not lack emotionally or in any other way, because he leads me to what I need. In times of hurt, he leads me to the place of tranquility (the still waters) to restore my mind, will, and emotions.

The Bible also describes someone who cares as the great high priest. He is described as one who can be touched by the emotions of our weaknesses (infirmities) and vulnerabilities. A bona fide caregiver is one who can identify with the one who is hurt. In this role, sympathy is not the remedy. The role here is to usher the hurting to his or her healing. When you are healed from your hurts, remember how dangerously you came to not recovering and sliding into a pit of self-pity and perpetual sorrow. The high priest was the only one who could enter into the holy of holies and commune with God directly. The nation of Israel was called "a kingdom of priests" (Exodus 19:6) and the church (1 Peter 2:5, 9) priesthood. God will use you as a priestly intercessor for someone who is hurting. We are guided by Scripture for the strong to bear the infirmities of the weak. If you are hurting, the ministry of intercessory prayer for others will become a healing agent for you too.

The role of the hurting is to approach the throne of grace with confidence (come boldly…). Grace is extended to everyone. His grace (favor) is sufficient. Confidence in the one who cares is needed because there is always the intimidation factor of past experiences. Confidence is needed in the ability of God to be God. Many of the scriptures we know and clichés we repeat are diminished when life is at its worst. Matthew recorded Jesus saying, "Come unto me, all ye that labour and are heavy laden, and I will give you rest. Take my yoke upon you, and learn of me; for I am meek and lowly in heart: and ye shall find rest unto your souls" (Matthew 11:29, KJV). Why work so hard carrying burdens? Anything too heavy ought to be laid down. Burdens begin to affect your ability to function. You need rest.

His advice is well stated: "Make my yoke." The yoke around the neck of the oxen was never designed to weigh the animal down. The yoke is a tool for giving direction. If what you are doing is not allowing you to go in a positive direction, lay it down. He is saying to take his direction by discarding yours. Exchange your direction for his (Jesus) and learn how to function again. Learn how to laugh as well as cry. Learn from the Word of God to strategies for life. The advice of the saged preacher comes to mind: "Trust in the Lord with all thine heart; and lean not unto thine own understanding. In all thy ways acknowledge him, and he shall direct thy paths" (Proverbs 3:5–6). Your faith in the Lord will be tested. Do not allow yourself to listen to you, but listen to the voice of the Lord in you. He will guide you safely to the next dimension of power and victory, because he is someone who cares.

# STANDING ON THE PROMISES OF GOD

Scripture Text: Matthew 14:25–29

Focus: Safety and Peace

The source of our faith will determine the extent of our success. If faith is in a limited source, our success will not reach far. If our faith is in God, success will be magnified. The Word of God is filled with promises from the Lord. This lesson will focus on the power of those promises to provide solid ground on which to stand.

One night, a terrible storm arose from the sea. It came at an unusual time. The five thousand, besides women and children, had completed their roadside dinner. The storm came in the midst of their ministering to the people. The disciples had simply been obeying the directives of Jesus. This is a reminder that storms will arise at any given place or time. Even when you are functioning well and in the will of God, a storm may arise. Storms come in the lives of the righteous as well as the wicked. No one is exempt.

The lake was only four or five miles wide. The boat was small. Jesus quickly made his disciples get into a boat and cross to the other side ahead of him while he sent the people away. After sending the people away, he went up a mountain to pray by himself. When evening came, he was there alone.

The boat, now hundreds of yards from shore, was being thrown around by the waves because it was going against the wind. So too in our own lives, storms will seem to come out of nowhere. Storms will brew in the home, at work, or in the pew—anywhere! Between three and six o'clock in the morning, Jesus came to them, walking on the sea. In the midst of the storm is where you will find Jesus. Most people will miss him because the storm is so demanding. In the midst of your storm, you must know that the Lord is there.

When the disciples saw him walking on the sea, they were terrified. They said, "It's a ghost!" and began to scream because they were afraid. Immediately, Jesus said, "Calm down! It's me. Don't be afraid!" Here is the comfort preceding the promise. In this human experience of storms, we often exhaust our strength running from storms or fearing them. But listen to Jesus saying, "Don't be afraid. It's me!" Hear him now in the midst of your storm. What does he say? Peter discovered the answer. Peter answered, "Lord, if it is you, order me to come to you on the water." Jesus said, "Come!"

So Peter got out of the boat and walked on the water toward Jesus. But when he noticed how strong the wind was, he became afraid and started to sink. He shouted, "Lord, save me!" Peter may be accused, and arguably so, for being impulsive and spontaneous because he got out of the boat. Perhaps this is the key to receiving the promises of God. Perhaps it is better to leap out of the boat by faith than to take so long in the boat that you never take the leap of faith and miss the promise. Immediately Jesus reached out, caught hold of him, and said, "You have so little faith! Why did you doubt?" When they got into the boat, the wind stopped blowing. The promise was fulfilled. Peter was safe in the presence of Jesus.

Even though the promise was made, Peter's eyes wavered from the source of his promise. Peter was a professional fisherman. He knew that men do not walk on water. When he stepped out of the boat onto the water, his faith was pure (unmixed). He was not standing on water but on the promise of Jesus. When faced with storms, you have to know where you are standing. When you are called by the Lord to step out of your comfort zone, what will you stand on? If you are on a spiritual or emotional seesaw, up and down, you need to hurry and get off and stand on the promises of God. If you are always stumbling through the same difficul-

Malcolm W. Coby, Ph.D.

ties time after time, you need to check where you are
standing. It may be the slippery ground of false promises of your own flesh.

Slippery places include doubt, fear, and worry. That
is always uncertain territory. There are times when you
want to stand but cannot see where to stand. How can
you justify standing when all is hopeless? How can you
possibly stand when you have never been able to stand
before? The answer is simple. Even if you need help
to stand, never been successful in standing, have fallen
time and time again, and even if you are sinking down
right now, stand firm on the promises of God.

Promises by man are made daily. We hear the good
intentions of our friends and loved ones. The husband
tells his wife, "I will be home for dinner at six, dear."
"I will pick you up at ten o'clock." "Wait for me. I will
be there on time." They sound genuine. People have
good intentions. However, those intentions are often
offset by their humanity. The tragedy is that reliance
on manmade promises can be disappointing. Broken
promises can result in broken dreams and broken
hearts. Dreams and expectations that are given life by
promises are attached to our emotions. Empty promises have no substance on which we can stand. They
are elusive. They lead to false hope. False hope can be
destructive to faith, because faith is the substance of
things hoped for.

On the other hand, the promises of God are certain. They are unfailing. We are encouraged to hold fast our profession of faith without wavering, because God is true to his word (promises). The promises of God are always on time, in spite of what we may think. Abraham believed the promise of God and stood on it until the promise was born. He certainly demonstrated faith, and it was accounted as righteousness on his behalf. What seemed to be a biological impossibility manifested itself as a divine fulfillment of the promise of God. And even when the promise was fulfilled, the challenge of God to offer his son, Isaac, to God did not nullify the promise. As Abraham ascended to the mountain to worship God by offering his only son as the sacrifice, Abraham's focus was on the credibility of God. He told the men that accompanied him and Isaac to the place of worship, "My son and I are going to the mountain to worship God, and we shall return." You have to know without a doubt that God will indeed provide wherever he guides. Stand on his Word. The Word of God will speak the promise with clarity. It is our job to trust that his own Word will accomplish that for which God sent it to accomplish. When you find your confirmation of a promise in Scripture, take a stand. As Paul taught (my paraphrase), "Stand therefore, having your loins [places of vulnerability] strengthened by the truth of God's word" (Ephesians 6:14).

Do not let your faith waver by situations and circumstances. Situations are those events that are new to your experience, whether you created them or not. Situations are often problematic. They present us with the choice of fight or flight. If you choose to flee, the situation will become a circumstance. Circumstances are circular events. They have been in your life before. They always return because you chose not to fight the good fight of faith and conquer them. Circumstances, by definition, are conditions that affect one's life and are beyond his or her control. However, I submit that the authority of the Word of God contradicts the definition. You often hear people say that they are doing well "under the circumstances." Under anything is no position for a believer unless it is under the blood of Jesus. The believer is assured that he is more than a conqueror through Jesus, the one who loves us.

Standing on the Word of God is a process involved in full deliverance and healing from situations and circumstances. You only stand where you have arrived. However you got there is not the issue. The issue is what you choose to stand on once you have arrived at the situation of a divorce, illness, grief, or whatever. Should you decide to stand on worry, fear, intimidation, depression, etc, you are standing on slippery ground. It will be just a matter of time before you fall. Should you decide to stand on the promises of the Word of God, prepare yourself for an incredible experience of development. The more you pray the promise and celebrate the promise, the stronger your spirit and mind will become. Stay right there until God gives you further directions. His word will be a lamp to your feet to show you where you are and a light to your path to give you direction for the next part of your journey. Stand on the promises of God.

# ENDNOTES

1  Kubler-Ross, Elizabeth, M.D., *On Death and Dying,* 1969, New York: Touchstone Publishers.

2  Temes, Roberta, *Living With An Empty Chair: A Guide Through Grief,* 1992, New Jersey: New Horizons Press.

3  Field, David: Family Personalities, 1988, Oregon: Harvest House Publishers.

4  Accordance 6.1, NIV *Dictionary,* Oaktree Software, Inc., January, 2004